"In *Money Makers*, recruiting v that recruiting is a sales job with .... ay around). The best professional recruiters sell the right opportunities to job candidates, and then the right candidates to hiring managers. Ruffini's approach to tackling one specific topic each week will help good recruiters become great and great recruiters become masterful at the profession. This book will be one of those rare texts that stay on your desk, becoming a ready-reference tool for best-in-class recruiting practices."
- Scott Wintrip, author of *High Velocity Hiring: How to Hire Top Talent in an Instant*, and President of the Wintrip Consulting Group

"Having trained over 10,000 recruiters in the last 30+ years, I am able to say with the utmost confidence that John Ruffini and his 52 excellent tips on the true art of recruiting are jam packed with superior training "nuggets of gold" that will guarantee your success! As the professional staffing industry continues to rapidly evolve in the use of technology, John's high touch principles of developing long-term, trust based relationships with candidates of today and tomorrow are the secrets you need to apply daily in order to consistently win in the very competitive game of recruiting. Whether you are a veteran recruiter or just starting your journey in our very rewarding industry, make the decision to follow John's steps and you will have tremendous impact on your candidates and clients, plus earn Bags of Money in process!!!"
- Tim Kelch, CPC, CEO Top Tier Consulting

"John has put together an outstanding, detailed, yet simple plan that will "Make you Money" in the recruiting industry. I have had the privilege of working with John for many years and he was one of the most consistent billers, year after year. As he says, not the highest and nowhere near the lowest, but always above average – during good times and bad! His tricks and methods simply work. John has laid them out for you in 52 sections, one for each week of the year. Read this book and you will make more money!"
- Neil Lebovits, CPA, CPC, CTS, Founder, TheDynamicSale.com

$$$

MONEY MAKERS

Proven Ways to Increase Sales and Productivity in the World of

Professional Recruiting

By John Ruffini

© 2016

$$$

For Lisa, my one constant in an

ever-changing and unstable world.

I love you.

$$$

CONTENTS

$$$

CONTENTS (*continued*)

INTRODUCTION

I am in sales. There, I said it. The first step is always admission, right? Never in my wildest dreams did I ever think I would end up in a sales position. Growing up I associated all sales people with used car salesmen. Unfair, yes, but I did not know differently. I was ignorant to the sales arena. I could never see myself walking door to door, making telemarketing calls during dinner hour, or selling anything. That was because I was tainted by the word 'sales.' I thought 'selling' meant you had to talk a person into buying something they did not want. Again, that was my ignorance. I knew sales professionals made a lot of money. When I was in the software industry, developing applications using software that our sales reps sold to clients, I was always in awe of their lifestyle. Flashy clothes, fancy cars, nice homes. So, while I was unfamiliar and, at the time, uninterested in 'sales,' I did notice that it was clearly a way to make a lot of money.

Then, in 1994, my opinion of sales, and my life, changed dramatically. I was hired into the recruiting industry. The funny thing was, even though I was being paid 100% on commission, and even though I had a monthly and annual quota to achieve I still did not consider what I was doing as 'sales.' I simply thought I was getting paid to find talented professionals for various companies. It wasn't until I was in the business several years that I had the self-realization that I was in sales. I had become exactly what I never thought I would be. And I loved it! I feel fortunate that I had (and still have) some great people in my personal and professional life to whom I looked as mentors. Professionally, I feel blessed to have started my recruiting career in an organization that, in my opinion, taught me great fundamental skills. They did not just teach me how to recruit. They instilled in me the importance and value of cultivating long term relationships. That is the key to any sales professional's long-term success, and it is especially true in any service-related sales career such as recruiting. I realized very quickly that if I did my job correctly, I never really had to 'sell' anything to anyone. If I did my job correctly, and worked smart, I would simply be giving people what they wanted. I also found that if I did end up 'selling' someone on an opportunity, I had more than likely not done my job correctly.

$$$

I am not the most successful recruiter that ever lived, nor have I made the most money. Thankfully, I have achieved great success, earned considerable income, and mentored many within the industry who have gone on to be wildly successful. That is from where the inspiration for this book evolved. I enjoy passing on what I have learned and helping the next generation of recruiters prosper. I also enjoy shedding new light on old topics to the tenured recruiting community; because as we all know, the longer we do something and the more successful we are, the more we become settled into our ways and forgetful of the job's most essential elements.

There is more than one approach to recruiting, and mine is one of them. The information contained in this book will help you be a better, more efficient and effective recruiter, regardless as to what it is you recruit for. The techniques, tools and tips contained within this book can be applied to any recruiting position, be it with a third-party agency, an internal corporate recruiter, or an independent recruiter who works for his or herself. Recruiters are sales professionals, and a driving reason why people get into sales is the opportunity to control your income. The key is learning how to master certain activities and techniques that will help you get there:

- Learning the basic fundamentals of the business,

- Staying true to them and expanding upon them,

- Pushing yourself to continue to learn new ways to make yourself and your team better.

That is exactly what the Money Makers contained in this book will do for you.

I have written hundreds of Money Makers in my career, and have selected 52 for you to start with and focus on – one for every week in the year. You see, when you read a self-help book, there is a tendency to want to put everything you have learned to work right away. That is simply not possible. You take one step at a time, integrating one element at a time, until you master it and are ready to integrate more. **That way you build and you don't forget.** That is how I want you to look at the Money Makers. Focus on implementing one per week, and build as you progress. The key is not to forget about the Money Makers you have already put into action. Rather, add to them. Focus on one at a time and LEAP forward (Learn, Evaluate, Advance, Perform). Learn the Money Maker. Put it into action and Evaluate its effectiveness. Once mastered, Advance to the next Money Maker. As a result, you will position yourself to perform at your highest capability. Money Makers will help you take that giant LEAP in productivity you need to achieve your greatest potential as a recruiter. **LEAP!** What's a good sales book without an acronym here and there, right?

Recruiting, at the core, is a very simple business. Recruiters themselves have a tendency to over complicate things. Keep it simple, learn and master the fundamentals, and don't try to reinvent the wheel. Adapt to changing times, yes. Integrate technology where appropriate to enhance operations, yes. But keep things simple.

I wish I could tell you that every call I made as a recruiter was perfect. Perfectly executed? Maybe sometimes. Perfect? uh...no. Who's perfect? What's perfect? I'll tell you what's perfect...as summertime approaches in the great state of Maryland where I live, thoughts stray to a bushel of Maryland blue crabs, some Old Bay seasoning, a little cider vinegar and a cold beverage...now THAT'S perfect...but I digress.

If every time you did something you did it perfectly, where would the challenge be? How would you grow, learn and get better? If you are perfect, you are as good as you are going to be. Nobody's perfect. And that's ok. The question is, when you fail, do you try again or do you lose confidence and give up. My advice to you would be the former (that would be the 'try again' one). Have a bad call? So what. Make another call. Make a bad intro at a networking event? So what. Go back over to that person and re-introduce yourself. Have a deal fail because you did not prep a candidate well enough? As unfortunate as that may be, learn from it and do a better job next time.

Michael Jordan was cut from his high school basketball team. He did not give up. Walt Disney was fired from a newspaper for 'lack of creativity.' He did not give up. Abraham Lincoln was defeated in numerous elections. He did not give up. Albert Einstein was told by his elementary school teacher that he had limited intelligence. He did not give up. Through failure, we all grow. It teaches us and makes us stronger. All of the aforementioned people ended up being the best (or one of the best) in their professions. Throughout their careers, they failed often, but they never gave up. And neither should you.

Take advice from Henry Ford who said that "failure is the opportunity to try again with more intelligence." I imagine Henry failed a few times before getting the automobile right. Good thing he kept trying.

If you never try, fail, and try again, you will never be the best you can be. Don't be afraid to fail. Take risks, take chances. Learn from your mistakes (and the mistakes of others) and keep trying. You will become better as a result!

As you read through this book, keep one very important thing in mind that applies to every Money Maker. For every conversation and meeting you have as a recruiter, here is a short and simple message that often goes overlooked:

- It's about them, not us.

- It's what's in it for them, not what's in it for us.

- It's about what they want, not what we want.

- It's about what they need, not what we need.

Everything we do...everything we say...every conversation we have has to focus on the candidate or the client. That is the key to building relationships and rapport. Remember this simple fact and you will set yourself apart from the competition.

Finally, remember that in sales, your raise is effective as soon as you are. This book, or rather the contents of it, will make you more effective.

Happy Hunting!

John

$$$

Terminology

Throughout this book I will use some terms that, depending on how long you have been in the business and where you work, may or may not sound familiar. So as not to confuse anyone, I wanted to take a moment to outline some of the terms you will see and how I am using them.

- **Send out:** This is when one of your candidates interviews with a client.

- **Company In:** This is when you invite one of your clients into your office for the purpose of interviewing several candidates your firm is representing.

- **Recruiting Vertical:** A particular area of specialization such as an industry (i.e. Finance & Accounting, Human Resources)

- **Demand Area:** Simply put, this represents candidates and job orders that are typically most 'in demand' in most markets, all the time. Each recruiting vertical has its own unique demand area.

- **Active Candidate (Actives):** These are candidates that are openly and actively seeking out new career opportunities. Their resumes can usually be found on job boards, and they are actively sending out resumes and interviewing for jobs.

- **Passive Candidate (Passives):** These are candidate who are currently employed and not actively or aggressively seeking new opportunities. Their resumes are not on job boards (if they even have a resume at all).

- **MPC:** Most Placeable Candidate. This is a profile of a candidate (yes, a real person – not made up) that will appeal to most managers in most markets most of the time. It is used to stimulate conversation in an effort to get a job order.

- **MVJO:** Most Viable Job Order. This is an overview of a job opportunity (yes, a real one, not made up) that will appeal to most candidates in most markets most of the time. It is used to stimulate conversation in an effort to recruit candidates

$$$

Money Maker #1: Plan Your Work...Work Your Plan!

The single most challenging and critical aspect in sales is planning. If you fail to plan, you should plan to fail. Planning your day sounds simple enough; but the problem is, there is no one single method for planning. There are numerous options, because planning is personal. You have to develop a method and style that works for you.

Planning. We hate to take the time to do it, but we all *need* to do it if we want to be successful. In the world of recruiting, it's all about control. Controlling the candidate, controlling the client, controlling the placement process... controlling time. Determining where and how you spend your time is one difference between a good recruiter and a great recruiter. Good recruiters work. Great recruiters work smart. They focus on activities that are closest to the money, and they do not allow themselves to be distracted by non-revenue generating activities. While they are at work, they....well.....work! They know what they have to do and they execute. They not only plan their work, they work their plan.

$$$

To make the most of everything you do and maximize your chances for success, you need to have a daily plan. That's right, daily. If you take the time to plan, you will get much more out of your days. Furthermore, planning is not simply writing a "to do" list. You need to drill down. You need to prioritize that list and determine which activities you "have to" accomplish and which would be "nice to" accomplish. Then take that list and time-block your day into chunks of activity, whereby each block is dedicated to a specific task. Within those time blocks, you need to have a prepared call plan. This is where you can really achieve exponential levels of productivity. You see, it's not enough to say you will be "recruiting" for a specific profile during a call block. When that call block arrives, you should have a prepared list of names and telephone numbers and be ready to dial. If you use the time during that call block to search for people to call, you will end up hunting and pecking around and will, at best, make about 5 calls in an hour. Why make 5 when you can make 20 or 30? Many calls will undoubtedly go directly voice mail on the initial attempt, so you need to plan how to get a lot out of a little window of opportunity. In the same light, if you are blocking out time to market a strong candidate, you should be ready and waiting with names and numbers of hiring managers. When you plan and execute in this fashion, you not only get more out of your day, you also allow yourself to get into a rhythm, because you are grouping similar calls together in the same block. The more you do something, the better you get at it. My high-level planning recommendations are as follows:

- Schedule candidate interviews and client meetings early in the morning, midday and late afternoon/early evening/after hours. You have to control when you will meet with candidates. Don't let them control you.

- Preserve the hours of 9am-11am and 2pm-4pm for outbound calling only – typically better times for recruiting and sales activities.

- Get in early and stay late. If not every day, a few days each week. Preserve the hours from 7am – 8:30am and 5:30pm – 7pm for outbound marketing calls. Most hiring managers are at their desks during those times and usually any assistant/gatekeeper is not, so there is a higher-percentage chance that they will answer their own phone. Catching them between 9am and 5pm is virtually impossible, so plan to attack them during off hours.

- Balance your plan. Don't plan to do just one thing all day (i.e. "Friday will be my reference check day"). That never pans out. Break your day up so that you have a variety of activities every day. It will keep you balanced and keep you fresh. Plan time to recruit, to market, and to interview candidates every day. Each day should include two candidate interviews, reference check calls, marketing calls and recruiting calls. Like Mr. Miagi said in *The Karate Kid*.....*"*Must have balance!" I think that is some ancient proverb or word of wisdom.....or maybe it was just some gymnastic coach yelling instructions to the kid on the balance beam.....but I digress. In our business, we must have balance. Balance of activity, that is. Maintaining a balanced

attack – a constant combination of marketing and recruiting –
is the best way to maximize your chances for long-term
success. There are times when we tend to react to the
market. There are days when you come into the office and
there are SO many job orders and NO candidates to present
to them, that you say to yourself, "All I am going to do this
week is recruit, because there are all these hot job orders and
I need to get candidates for them." And so you will. You
will do nothing but recruit….for a week…and maybe you
will land some strong recruits and present them, or maybe
you will not. Come next week, you will say to yourself,
"Wow, I have all these solid candidates, now I need job
orders to place them in. All I am going to do this week is
market." And you will. You will do nothing but market…all
week…and maybe you will land some job orders that are
right for those newly-found candidates or maybe you will
not. And this cycle will repeat and spiral into oblivion if you
are not careful. The key is to never let this cycle

start. Regardless of how many job orders and how many solid candidates you have (and by the way, you can NEVER have too many good ones of either), you should maintain a balance of recruiting and marketing in your daily plan. **Do both. Every day.** Recruiters get paid to deliver talent to clients. Because of that, we should be recruiting for talent every day - talent we need for current job orders and talent that exist in our space in general, whether we have an opportunity for them right now or not. The latter would be inventory recruiting, and that is something that we should constantly be doing. We should be meeting with passive candidates (recruits) as well as active candidates (from job boards) every day. We should also be marketing every day. We should be making "hunting" marketing calls (to companies we know are looking to hire right now) and "farming" marketing calls (to companies where we believe there is future business to be had). We should be meeting with clients every day, whether they have current needs or not. Being proactive is a much better way to operate. When you are proactive and ~~you~~ are constantly recruiting and marketing every day, you will develop a vast network of clients and candidates. Your pipeline will grow exponentially. Don't fall off the balance beam! Maintain balance….in your daily plan, that is.

$$$

Sample Recruiter Daily Plan

7:30am – 9:00am	Time used for the following: Client Visit, Candidate Interview, internal team meeting and check voice mail / email Also use this time for outbound marketing calls
9:00am – 9:45am **On the phone**	Reference Check Calls, Job Board (Active Candidate) calls - have them listed out prior, names and numbers
9:45am – 10:00am	Documentation, use restroom, refill coffee, etc.
10:00am – 10:45am **On the phone**	Candidate Reconnect Calls - have them listed out prior, names and numbers (see Money Maker #6)
10:45am – 11:00am	Documentation, use restroom, refill coffee, etc.
11:00am – 11:30am	Check and return email and voice mail
11:30am – 1:30pm	Time used for the following: Candidate Interview, Client Visit/Lunch
1:30pm – 2:00pm	Check and return email and voice mail
2:00pm – 2:45pm **On the phone**	MPC (recruiting calls to passive candidates) or MVJO (marketing) Calls - have them listed out prior, names and numbers of hiring managers or candidates
2:45pm – 3:00pm	Documentation, use restroom, refill coffee, etc.
3:00 – 3:45pm **on the phone**	Inventory Recruiting Calls – for demand area talent or a job order you need to recruit for
3:45pm – 4:00pm	Documentation, use restroom, refill coffee, etc.
4:00pm - 5:30pm	**PLANNING** (for the next day)
5:30pm – 7:00pm	Time used for the following: Candidate Interview, Client Meeting over drinks/dinner

$$$

The end of your day can fluctuate. For instance, you may have a candidate interview at 4:30pm or 5:00pm which will push your planning later into the day. In the beginning, you may need to budget as much as 90 minutes for planning. This will get shorter as you evolve and get comfortable. As a point of reference, when I entered this business, I worked 7:30am-7:30pm consistently for my first year and some Saturdays. I knew I had to invest the time if I was going to master the business.

Ours is an interruption-driven business. When your plan gets interrupted – and it will - by something that is of a higher priority (closer to the money); abandon your plan and attack the interruption. When it is handled, return to your plan from that point on, and move all unfinished activities to another day's plan. If you have a plan to return to, you are in good shape. When you do not, things can get really crazy and confusing.

If you consistently plan, you put yourself in a position to win. With this in mind, you need to understand the **'WIN'** principle -

What's Important Now. Yes, it's another acronym in a world cluttered by them. Sorry….not really sorry….but I digress.

In our world, there are a lot of moving parts and a lot of potential distractions that can cause us to lose focus. The key to success is to be disciplined enough to ignore the distractions and recognize which activities you should be focusing on and accomplishing (i.e., the ones that will make you money). Know **What's Important Now**! Try not to worry about or be distracted by what your competition is doing, how they are doing it or what they are doing differently from you. Focus on your own performance - what you can control. And make sure you are always doing **What's Important Now.**

Every day, and throughout the day, ask yourself, "**What's Important Now?**" If you find that you are not focusing on the activities and events that are most critical to your success, take that opportunity to re-focus yourself. Make sure you have planned out your day, every day, and within that plan, have a call plan designed to work closest to the money (short-term), as well as one that builds for the future (long-term). Constantly strive to improve your craft. Little by little, you will find yourself honing skills, working more and more on **What's Important Now**, and as a result, gaining the respect of your clients, candidates and peers.

And when it comes to going up against your competition? You will win if you focus on the **WIN**!

Commit to planning. Some days will be better planned than others, but if you are committed to planning, more than not you will be in control of your day. You can use a Day-Timer, Franklin Planner, Outlook, Google Calendar, smartphone, database planner, Excel spreadsheet....even a pad of paper and a pencil. Whatever tool works best for you, use it. I don't care what tool you use to plan, as long as you plan! **Plan your work....work your plan!**

$$$

Money Maker #2: Know Your Sweet Spot - Your 'Demand Area'

Work smart, not hard. That is a phrase that every professional has heard a thousand times, and all too often we don't heed the message. In the business of recruiting, businesses pay for talent. And while at times they may have critical needs in very specific areas within their organization, there are certain talent profiles that are, for the most part, always in the highest demand. Always. These are professionals that hiring managers will always want to look at - regardless if there is a broadcasted opening or not - and potentially hire them. Because they always need them. These are talent profiles referred to as 'demand area' profiles. And just what is the demand area profile? It depends on what your recruiting area of specialization is. If you specialize in Accounting & Finance placements, for example, your demand area is Staff Accountant, Senior Accountant, and Financial Analyst. Companies are always hiring those profiles. In Human Resources, Generalists, Recruiters, and HR Managers typically seem to be in consistent high demand. Sales & Marketing recruiters may want to zero in on Sales Reps,

Account Executives, and Sales Managers. And in the world of Information Technology, Software Developers are always needed. If you do not fall into one of those recruiting verticals, your job is to figure out what your demand area is. Trying to be all things to all companies is an impossible task. If you specialize in an area, it is critical to know what your demand area is; because it will make your life a bit easier. You will work smarter, always spending the majority of your recruiting and marketing efforts within the demand area. **Demand area job orders + demand area candidate inventory = $$$$$!**

$$$

Money Maker #3: Use Scripts. Make Your Life Easier!

To Script or not to Script….that is the question! Shakespeare had a *different* question, but Shakespeare was not a recruiter, at least to my knowledge…but I digress.

Scripts. Some use them, some don't. Some like them, some don't. Some think they sound salesy, some don't. Some recruiters are so experienced and smooth at their delivery that they have scripts committed to memory and don't necessarily "need" to have them written down. Using scripts is a very opinionated issue. Personally, I am always of the mindset that if there is a tool that can make my job easier and, in effect, not tax my brain as much, why not use it? A script has that impact and to this day, 20+ years into the recruiting business, I still use a script if I am making marketing or recruiting calls. A script guarantees a quality call. It guarantees a smooth delivery. It separates you from your competition. It guarantees a solid first impression when making a phone call to an unknown (or known) audience…and we all know what they say about first impressions.

$$$

As recruiters, we make an enormous number of phone calls on a daily basis (well, we *should*, anyway). Most of these calls are either of a recruiting or marketing nature (or both!). When making calls, you introduce yourself, mention something attractive about the candidate or job you are marketing (often referred to as 'sizzle'), and then you hope to enter into a dialogue. Unfortunately, when not using a script, that first, all-important part (intro and sizzle) is often inconsistent. When you have it scripted out in front of you, you never have to worry about what you are going you say; you just need to focus on how you are going to say it. That's much easier than having to think on the fly and make up new verbiage on every call….when you are banging out hundreds of calls! Having a script also eliminates all those "ums" and "uhs" that are inevitable if you are thinking on the fly.

To avoid sounding robotic, write your script in words that are natural for you. Write it as if you were talking face to face with someone in a conversation. Tailor it to your style. Remember, a powerful script has three parts: An introduction (who you are, what you do and the purpose of your call), the body (containing 3-5 strong sizzle points about either your candidate or your job order….and remember, these are qualities that would excite the person on the other end of the phone, not a candidate's daily job duties or a job description) and a close (an open-ended question – one where the person on the other end of the phone has to provide more than a simple "yes/no" response – designed to open a dialogue). Your script should be no longer than 30 seconds in length when delivered at a normal speaking pace.

Remember, the goal of every phone call we make is to have a business conversation and obtain information. Where each call eventually ends up taking us is unknown. If we never get to the dialogue, however, the call will not lead us anywhere. A powerful script maximizes your chances for getting to that dialogue. Write scripts. Practice them. Get on the phone and use them. You will be amazed at how much easier they make your job and how much more professional you sound on the phone.

To Script or not to Script? You tell me……

$$$

Money Maker #4: Qualify In, Not Out...Don't Make Value Judgments!

As recruiters, we get paid to deliver talent. Often times, however, we get in our own way and overlook talent that can add value to our business and, more importantly, our clients. When recruiting, we need to continually cast our net wide. Our job is to network - to talk to as many individuals in our vertical area of expertise as possible. The more people we speak to, the more people we speak to! That being said, when evaluating a candidate's resume or profile and deciding whether or not to get on the phone and/or meet with that person, try not to be overly critical or analytical. Don't overthink things. When in doubt, get them on the phone. Network with them. Build rapport and get reference and referral information. Every person is a potential candidate or client, be it now or in the future; and every person is a source for information and referrals that can help grow your business. Yes, we need to deliver quality to our clients. In order to get to the quality, we need to have quantity, and that is what we sometimes forget. Get people into *your* system and make them work for *you*. Your clients do a good enough job of qualifying candidates out. You need to qualify people in, not out!

I was talking to a recruiter recently and heard something I hear often. They told me that their interview numbers were light because the people they were finding did not fall in line with any of the jobs they were currently looking to fill; and because of that, they were not bringing them in. This is a catastrophic mistake in our world. We have to remember that as recruiters, our job is to constantly recruit for talent, not just for job orders. It is easy to do the latter simply because everything in our world is focused on send outs and starts. However, remember these key facts:

- Every sub-par candidate has worked for excellent managers
- Every sub-par manager has supervised excellent employees

Think long term. Think network. Think residual pay off. As the old saying goes, our job is a marathon not a sprint. So it is not always about what can you do for me today, or what have you done for me lately....80's Janet Jackson reference there....but I digress...it's about what information can I get today that will benefit my desk at some point. And we never know when that benefit will come. But it *will* come. It always does.

Additionally, once you have talent in your hands, be careful not to make value judgments. When evaluating talent, remember that *you* are not the hiring manager. You are not interviewing these candidates to work for you. Therefore, you cannot rule out candidates that *you* don't think measure up for intangible reasons. If a candidate is technically qualified, present them to your hiring manager. Granted, there are candidates that you know without a doubt would not be right for an opportunity. I am not talking about them. I am referring to the numerous times when there is a gray area....when a candidate falls in line with the requirements of a job but you're just not sure about one or two things (personality, job history, etc.). Those are the times you need to let the *client* decide. If you do not present those individuals, your competition will. As long as you position the presentation professionally, and explain (a) why you are presenting the person, (b) what the potential negatives might be perceived by the client and (c) that you wanted to let the client have the opportunity to review the candidate profile and decide for themselves, you will not lose respect from your client. If you simply submit a resume or profile that is out of line with what your client asked for without that dialogue, you will. Therein lies the difference. It's all how you position it. Apply this same approach with your candidates. If there is an opportunity that is not *exactly* what a candidate said they *ideally* wanted, but has much of what they desire, you should be discussing that opportunity with the candidate - allowing *them* to decide if they want to explore it or not. One of the worst feelings in this business is finding out that a candidate of *yours* was just placed by a competitor into a job that *your* team had on the books but *you* didn't think was good enough to show to the client. You simply cannot afford to make those value judgments.

In our world, we can definitely control two things….time and information. We can control who we talk to, who we interview, and with whom we interact and network. We can control the questions we ask, who we ask them to and what we do with the information we gather from the answers. The more people we talk to, the bigger our network. No matter how many people you have talked with and/or met, there are always more out there in the market to touch. Make this year the year you expand your network exponentially. To do that, simply follow the formula **Success = IN^3**.

If a person is **IN** your space....and **IN** your market...they need to be **IN** your book of business.

If they are not IN your book, they will be IN someone else's....most likely your competitor's! So cast your net wide. Don't pre judge or qualify out. Qualify in. Everyone knows someone. Everyone is a link to a potential new candidate or client. So get them IN the door and IN your book.....and you will be IN the know!

Success = IN^3 .... Commit to it!

Talk to more people, not less. Qualify in, not out....and take the blinders off. Think outside the box. Don't make value

$$$

judgments! Put these concepts into play and you will end up closing

a couple of deals that you otherwise would not have!

Money Maker #5: Don't Ignore Active Candidates!

Passive candidates. We need them. We crave them. We hunt them down daily. We do this because as recruiters, the passive candidate is the most "fee worthy" candidate and that is exactly what we should be delivering to our clients. Passives get recruited. Passives are not on the job boards. Clients typically cannot access passives, so they are willing and excited to pay recruiters a fee for them. We need the passive candidates. So what happens to the active ones? What about all those candidates actively seeking employment, plastering the inter-web with their resume, applying to every related (and unrelated) job posting they come across.....what about them? Some would argue those are great temp candidates. While that may be true, perm recruiters cannot, and should not, ignore the active candidate. Why? Because those candidates are on the market. They are actively seeking employment. Whether they are employed currently or not, they are out there. In your market. Interviewing. And you need to know where. You need to know with whom they are meeting. You need to be aware of their activity so that you can better understand your market, gather leads that can improve your desk activity, and ultimately generate GP….and money in your pocket!

Each week, perm recruiters spend most of their recruiting time pursuing passive candidates…and they should That being said, I encourage you to interview at least one – yes, one….singular….that's not asking too much – active candidate per day. Make sure the candidate is in your demand area (i.e., has a background or title that is most in-demand by the companies in your market). While we may not be able to place these people today, they might represent a future placement. Or, even better, they might end up in a decision-making position and be a future client. Regardless, we need to interview them now in order to begin to foster a relationship, gain market knowledge, references and referrals. Get leads. Find out where they have sent their resume, to what job opportunities, at what companies, where they have interviewed, names of hiring managers they have interviewed with, and more. If they are ~~still~~ actively involved in a placement cycle, we should not interfere. That would be unethical. However, if they are no longer active in a placement cycle, for whatever reason, we should be pursuing those leads aggressively and marketing our strongest candidates into those companies.

We place passive candidates. That is where we truly add value to our clients – by delivering talent they cannot access on their own accord. We need the active candidates for leads. Leads turn into job orders – job orders that we can then market our best passive candidates into. It's all about balance. Don't ignore the active candidate!

$$$

Money Maker #6: Doing Unselfish Things for Selfish Reasons:
The Candidate Recon Call!

If done completely and effectively, the candidate reconnect
(recon) call is an invaluable tool for recruiters. These are calls made
to ACTIVE candidates (ideally within your demand area) that you
have already interviewed, met with or done a qualifying call
with. Yes, it is a follow-up call with a candidate who, in most cases,
is not "fee worthy" at the present time for one reason or
another. That does not, however, mean the call is a waste of your
time. This is an activity that emulates the phrase, "We do unselfish
things for selfish reasons." On the surface, this is a very unselfish
call. It is a call to a candidate for which we do not have any
opportunities for at the current time. However, it is a call from
which we can learn and gain an awful lot of market information in
the form of job leads and referrals. THAT'S the selfish part. This
should not be a rushed call and necessarily a quick call. It should be
a two-way dialogue and recruiters should follow a structured flow in
order to make the most of the call. Remember, this is about getting

information…and information is what leads you to money! If these active candidates are interviewing with companies in your market, you need to know about it. You need to know what companies they are pursuing, when they interviewed, for what position, through whom (on their own, via a job board, via a recruiter or other), who the hiring manager is, if they are interested in the opportunity, and if they are still actively engaged in the interview process…..any and all information you can gather.

There are 5 key steps to an effective candidate recon call that will guarantee you will **LEARN** something from it (you knew there had to be an acronym in here somewhere, right?):

1. Show them a little **Love**! Tell the candidate you are calling to let them know that while you may not have anything for them at the present time, you have not forgotten about them. This alone will separate you from your competition and will impress the candidate. Remember, the number one complaint about recruiters from all candidates is that they

never hear from them after their initial conversation or meeting. At this point, the call is about them.

2. Review and re-confirm the candidate's personal **Expectations** - what they are looking for in the market. This shows that during your initial (or previous) conversation, you actually listened to them. At this point, the call is about them.

3. Review and re-cover any **Activity** they shared with you the last time you spoke with them (where they had been interviewing, sending resumes, etc.). It is important that you take notes each time you speak with the candidate so that you can refer to the information they shared with you on future calls. If they are still active in those loops, do not interfere. If they are not, however, those are job order leads you can pursue immediately!

4. Inquire about any **Recent** activity they have had in the market since your last discussion. Here is when the call shifts from just about them to about them AND you.

5. Source them for **New** candidate referrals for opportunities for which you are recruiting and for which they would not qualify ~~for~~ or be interested in. Always ask "Who do you know?" Whenever possible, paint a picture and be as specific as possible as to what you are sourcing for. For example, "At your last employer, when you needed help with a financial model who would you go to?" By being specific, you increase your chances for getting a referral.

This type of call is one that over time, unfortunately, often falls by the wayside for most recruiters. We often only concentrate on the passive candidates and while those are indeed the ones for whom our clients pay handsomely, we need to remember that it is important to not ignore the active candidates. Reconnect with them. It is recommended you connect with them on a weekly basis until either (a) they have found a new opportunity or (b) you no longer are getting any useful information from them. When making your daily plans, include the candidate recon call every

$$$

day. **LEARN** about your market from those who are actively

sending out resumes and interviewing.

$$$

Money Maker #7: Reference Checks: The Easiest Call You Will Ever Make!

Reference checks are, arguably, the easiest and warmest calls a recruiter can make. They are calls that people will take, calls that will be returned, and calls that will guarantee a conversation. They are the consummate lead-generator in our business - every one of them is a potential candidate or client! Yet, for some reason, they are also the calls that recruiters put on the back burner and only seem to make when they "need" to. My line of thinking is you **need** to make them every day. Every candidate you interview should be providing you with a list of references. When you get them, immediately put them on your call plan. Make yourself check 5 or more references daily on your candidates.

There are a number of reasons why we check references. Obviously, from a legal standpoint, you should never send a candidate to an interview with one of your clients without having at least one solid reference completed on that candidate (can you say liability?). That being said, at the end of every reference check call is an opportunity to engage in a dialogue that could lead to a candidate or client (or both!) relationship. To help set the call up at the beginning, say, "To put the call into perspective, could you please tell me a little about yourself, what you currently do, and what your professional relationship is or was with <candidate name>." The reference's response to that will dictate how you transition the call at the end. First conduct a comprehensive reference check on the candidate. It is an opportunity to show them your professionalism and how you do business. THEN transition into a conversation about them.....try to recruit them, market a candidate to them or just simply inquire about how their business is doing.

Reference checks are money making calls. If we are not making these calls daily, we are leaving money on the table.

Money Maker #8: Suggest Action. Be Confident!

Human nature. There are many things that fall into the category of "human nature." One of them is how we respond to certain things. The mind reacts differently based on how something is said or delivered. When *asked* a direct question, the mind tells us to first absorb, analyze, process and then respond with an answer. When *told* to do something from someone who has a tone of authority, the mind tends to tell us to....well....do it! When the mind perceives weakness or uncertainty, it tells us to question everything, probe for information and get defensive. Keep all that in mind when you are on the phone with candidates, clients, gatekeepers....everyone!

Suggest Action, don't ask for permission.

What sounds better and more confident to you in the following scenarios in which a recruiter is talking to a potential candidate?

a) "Your background is outstanding. I suggest we get together so that I can understand you more than on paper, learn more about what is important to you and your career, and determine what, if any, opportunities might make sense for you now or in the future."

b) "Your background is outstanding. Would you mind coming in to meet me for an interview?"

c) "Your background is outstanding. I'd like to possibly meet and maybe get to know each other better if that would be ok with you. It would kinda be better and we sorta have to meet in order to maybe, well, you know, place you into a position that is possibly a good fit for you."

If you voted for "A" you are correct. (if you voted for "C," please go to the principal's office for detention!)

What sounds better and more confident in the following scenarios when we are talking with a receptionist or another employee and trying to obtain the name of a controller at a company?

a) "Hi. Could you please tell me the name of your controller?"

b) "Tell me – who's your controller?"

c) "Hi. I was wondering if you could possibly tell me the name of the person who does the hiring for your accounting department."

If you voted for "B" you are correct. Be commanding. If you "tell" someone to do something, you'd be surprised how many times they simply do it without asking questions. "A" might cause a gatekeeper to question why you need the name. If you voted for "C"… again, please report to the principal.

Which sounds better and more confident when talking to a client about potential candidates in consideration?

a) "These candidates are the best the market has to offer. The market has become very competitive. I suggest we schedule a time when you can meet all three candidates back to back, immediately evaluate and compare, and thus guarantee you have a shot at hiring the one you want."

b) "Would you possibly be interested in meeting with any of the three candidates we've submitted?"

c) "Sure….take your time….all three candidates are passive and not going anywhere and we can schedule them in whenever it works for you. So it's no problem that you want to spread the meetings out over the course of the next month."

Clearly, "A" is more confident, more direct, and more authoritative. "B" is not necessarily incorrect, but it does not command the respect "A" does nor does it put you as the recruiter in control. If you voted for "C" …..by now you know the drill.

Confidence is your ally.

Confidence is embraced.

Confidence is rewarded.

Weakness is stepped on.

Be confident….and stomp out your competition!

$$$

Money Maker #9: Multi-Purpose Every Call!

Every person we talk to as recruiters is either a potential candidate or a potential client. We know this, but how often do we act upon it? When we enter into a conversation, there is usually one main objective to the call. Maybe we are targeting a candidate recruit, maybe we are trying to break into an account and land a job order, or maybe we are conducting a reference check. Regardless, we need to be aware of our target audience and be prepared to get the most out of every phone call. If we enter into a call with one objective and we achieve only that one objective, as a recruiter we have failed. There is SO much information to garner from every phone call and most of us tend to end telephone conversations too early. Information is our lifeline. Without it, we are useless. We need to aggressively pursue it on every call!

The MPC (Most Place-able Candidate) and MVJO (Most Viable Job Order) are your best weapons for accomplishing this and can usually be applied on every call.

For example, if you are recruiting for a position that has you calling candidates at a hiring manager level within organizations, start the call with an MVJO (a recruiting call). Pitch the job; see if you get a "nibble" on your bait. If you do, great! If not, don't end there. Get to know the person on the other end of the phone. Who are they? What do they do? How long have they been in their current company? Who do they know? ...you get the idea. Start compiling information! Then, and here's the part I love, remember that you are talking with a hiring manager. End the call with an MPC (a marketing call)! Something as simple as, "Oh, by the way, I am currently working with an exceptional candidate who <insert strong candidate sizzle here>" can lead to yet another whole conversation.

If you are making MPC calls trying to get job orders, whether your prospect "nibbles" on your MPC bait or not, start asking questions and gathering information! Remember...the person asking the questions is the one who is in control of the conversation. Then, before you end the call, use that same, "Oh, by the way...." Deliver a strong MVJO with sizzle that might catch the attention of your audience or turn it into an opportunity in which they provide you someone with whom you can network in the future.

Challenge yourself to extend the conversation, get information and multi-purpose every call!

$$$

Money Maker #10: Who, What, When, Where, Why, How….and Who Do You Know?

Questions, questions, questions. As recruiters, we ask a ton of them every day, in every conversation and with everyone we speak to. We crave information. Without it, we cannot do our job. To get information, we need to ask questions….and often, more than just questions that solicit a one-word answer. Open-ended questions (those that cannot be answered with a "yes/no" response) are often a key element in extending conversations and uncovering much needed information. Too often, we tend to rush through conversations and forget to ask important questions. Even if we do remember to ask them, we do not always get the true, detailed answer we need to do our job effectively. To illustrate this point, consider the following hypothetical dialogue between recruiter and candidate:

Recruiter: **Why** did you leave your last position?

Candidate: There was a reduction in force. (the recruiter *could* end it here and move on to the next question, but the best recruiters will probe deeper....)

Recruiter: I'm sorry to hear that. **When** did that happen?

Candidate: Last week.

Recruiter: I see. **Why** was there a reduction?

Candidate: Economic reasons. The company is shutting down.

Recruiter: That's unfortunate. **How** many were let go?

Candidate: A lot. Several hundred across the company including most of the department in which I work....and this is only the first phase.

Recruiter: **Where** within the company is this happening? Is this only at your office location or were other geographic areas impacted as well?

Candidate: Across the whole company. Locations in four states were hit. Maryland, Florida, Minnesota and California.

Recruiter: **What** has the company done to assist those that were let go?

Candidate: They gave us severance pay based on tenure with the company.

Recruiter: **What** was your severance package?

Candidate: 6 weeks' pay and benefits.

Recruiter: **Who** at the company would I speak with about seeing if our firm could help others like you during this transition period?

Candidate: Bill Jones, the COO would be the best person to speak with. He is running things.

Recruiter: Great – thank you. By the way, of those being let go, **Who Do You Know** that is strong with financial statement preparation? I am currently recruiting for an opportunity involving that and would like to network with people who have that skill.

Candidate: Well, Mary Johnson was our best in that area. She is still here but I think she will be let go in the next phase of reductions.

Recruiter: **When** is the next phase slated for?

Candidate: I think in another couple of weeks.

Recruiter: **What** is Mary's telephone number?

Candidate: You can call the main number and ask for extension 275.

Recruiter: Thank you.

If the recruiter simply accepts the candidate's reason for leaving and does not probe, look at all the information that would have been missed. Leads, leads, leads! We simply cannot stop at the surface in any situation. We need to extend the conversation and we can do that by continuing to ask probing, open-ended questions. Here's a simple recipe for information gathering:

- Ask a question, preferably an open-ended one.
- Be quiet. Let the other person answer the question. Resist the natural human tendency to suggest possible answers.
- Listen to their response.
- Acknowledge their response and leverage it into yet another open-ended question to probe deeper and deeper until you feel you've exhausted that item/topic.
- Repeat as necessary.

$$$

Remember, we have complete control over two things: time and information. We need to spend our time wisely gathering the right information. If we do that, we will be able to do our jobs much better and with a greater deal of confidence and control.

$$$

Money Maker #11: Follow-up...The Lost Art of recruiting!

Don't call us, we'll call you. But do we ever really call? The number one gripe among candidates and clients when it comes to recruiters is follow-up (or the lack thereof). Many times we shoot ourselves in the foot....we over promise and under deliver (as opposed to the opposite). We tell people we will call them...how often we will call them....when we will call them....and then we don't call. We tell clients we have candidates....great candidates.....that we're very confident we can fill their need....and then we don't present a single one. We are often our own worst enemy.

With respect to candidates....

Recruiters cannot place everyone. It would be great if we could, but we can't, and we don't. And it's ok (in fact, recommended) to let every candidate you meet with know this. As recruiters, we can help them in many ways, even if we do not place them. Many times, all candidates want is to be heard and to feel their recruiter generally cares about them. Here's a suggestion that will separate you from your competition: Get a stack of note cards and keep them at your desk. As soon as you finish interviewing a candidate, be it in person or long-lines (over the telephone, Skype, Google Hangout, etc.), send them a hand-written note **(NOT an email!)** that says, "Thank you for the opportunity to assist with your search." Include a couple business cards with the note and drop it in the outgoing mail same day. Then, a day or two after they interview with you, the candidate receives a hand-written note from you as a follow up, which makes a very favorable impression and functions as immediate follow-up. This is a very small action that has a powerful impact. Sending an email is ok, but not as personal. Another suggestion would be to keep a "hot list" of candidates that you want to stay close to, and physically include them in your daily call plans. It forces you to follow-up and stay in contact with them, but you control *who* and *when* you follow-up. This is critical for relationship building. Finally, when candidates call or email to check in, return the call....return the email. It makes a difference to them and it takes little time to do so. I cannot tell you how many referrals I have had over the years from candidates I did not place, simply because I was the one recruiter who always took their call, returned their call, returned their email and simply listened.

With respect to clients….

If we take a job order and sign a business agreement, we are committing to recruiting and delivering talent to a client. Sometimes we write job orders that we know very well we will never have candidates for, and sometimes we write very good job orders that we end up not filling for one reason or another. So, my first suggestion is to take thorough job orders and evaluate where you want to spend your time. Once you've done that, communicate with your client. We tend only to reach out to hiring managers when we present candidates, prep for interviews, debrief after interviews, etc….in other words, when *we* want or need something. Change that. If you are working a search, call your client weekly to see how things with the search are going - even if you personally have not presented candidates. Let them know your successes and challenges and what you are seeing in the market. Be consultative. Always ask them if there is anything else you could be doing for them. Another suggestion would be to email useful information to hiring managers in your market – whether they are active clients, prospects or other – on a bi-weekly basis. Find an article of interest from an online vehicle (CFO.com, Businessweek.com, ERE.net, or your local Business Journal/Crains are just a few helpful resources for this…there are many sites to choose from that will have information that most hiring managers will find interesting and/or useful) and sent it to them. *Give* them something instead of always *taking* or *selling*. It will be well received and appreciated. Throughout my career I did this religiously and as a result became a "go-to" guy for many managers in my market when it came to employment-related information, whether they were my client or not.

Communication is central to our business. Without it, relationships are hard if not impossible to foster. Try to do little things that involve a minimal investment of your time and make a maximum impact on your network. Respond to emails. Take phone calls. Return messages. It will come back to you tenfold and you

$$$

will clearly be different in the eyes (and ears) of the person on the other end of that communication!

Follow-up. It is many a recruiter's demise. Don't let it be yours.

$$$

Money Maker #12: Be Different....Pick Up the Phone!

OMG! LOL! IDK ....so goes today's world of

communication. It has become all too easy to email, text or IM

someone, that the art of communication is in jeopardy. Our clients

LOVE email. How often do we have clients tell us to communicate

through email only? It's frustrating. In our business, branding is

critically important – both a corporate brand AND an individual

brand. What is YOUR brand? How do you want to be

perceived? Remember, perception is reality. Technology is an asset

and can definitely improve your business operations, but use it

appropriately and wisely. Unfortunately, text-based communication

is often misinterpreted, ESPECIALLY WHEN YOU SHOUT (all

caps). People read emails and immediately form an opinion, get

defensive, get confused....so what do they do? They email right

back.....and THAT email gets misinterpreted....and the other person

gets defensive, irritated, confused.....and sends ANOTHER email

back......and my advice in most situations that involve or demand

direct communication with another live human being is simply *pick up the phone.* Yes, email and other electronic text-based communication vehicles are ok in many instances, but not when it involves critically-important dialogue such as pitching, prepping, debriefing, negotiating, closing....you get the point. Even if you get the other person's voice mail and have to leave a message, pick up the phone and call them. Have that direct VERBAL communication that is needed at critical points in the placement/sales cycle.

This is yet another very simple way to differentiate yourself from most of your competitors and to assert more control over your desk. You can tune in much better to a verbal conversation than you can to an email. Emails can also get you in trouble....so a few simple words of advice on that:

- Text for scheduling. Email for information (documents, etc.). Pick up the phone to persuade. I learned that from one of the best mentors and trainers in the recruiting business, Danny Cahill.

- Never write anything in an email, text or IM that you would not want printed on the front page of your local newspaper or posted on social media. Everything is backed up somewhere. Remember that. Yes, even Snapchat has backup servers!

- Never use email, text or IM for venting frustration...to anyone.

- Don't hide behind a keyboard. Become a real person to everyone you interact with in your job (and life, for that matter). Let them get to know you. After all, people buy from people they know and like, and how much can you *really* know and like someone if you never speak with them?

- Finally, for inter-office communications.....if you need to ask a teammate a question, pitch a candidate for a job order or have a discussion with them of any kind, get up, walk over to them and talk to them. Do NOT send an email when they are 10 or 20 feet away from you. I mean, really?

Be different. Pick up the phone. TTFN!

$$$

Money Maker #13: Be Careful What You Ask For….You Just Might Get It!

Recruiting (and all sales for that matter) is a business of asking questions, obtaining information and processing that information for the benefit of all. Often, however, it's the "asking questions" piece of our business that we cut corners on. We continually need to ask questions that go beneath the surface in order to gain a better understanding of what we are dealing with (so that we can best manage the situation). And it goes beyond that. Sometimes we fail to ask simple questions for fear that the answer might not be what we want – or even worse, might be what we *do* want!

Here are a few key questions / things we should be asking that sometimes go overlooked:

- ***Who do you know?*** (This question should be a staple in EVERY conversation you have as a recruiter)

- ***Why?*** (such a simple one-word question that can yield a ton of useful information)

- ***I'd like to have an exclusive on this search.*** (even if it is a 2-week exclusive, it can give you a leg up on your competition)

- ***I'd like to take you to lunch on Friday, talk about how things are going and, while I am there, pick up a check for the placement I just made with you.*** (At the end of the placed candidate's first week…you'd be surprised how often this will work!)

- ***Are you confident that either of your top two candidates would succeed in the job?*** (when you have the top two candidates moving to a final stage, if you can position it with your client that they should be prepared to hire EITHER candidate, you improve your chances for filling that job exponentially)

- ***I'd like you to take your resume off the job boards.*** (even if only for a couple weeks, so that your clients cannot find the resume on their own, should it be out there)

- ***Can you get me a company directory/phone list?*** (You've just placed a candidate. Chances are, there are more people like them at the company they are leaving. Take them to

lunch, celebrate the new career move and ask them to bring a

company directory with them while they are at it)

- ***Who should I start at quarterback this week in my fantasy***

   football game? (ok, so maybe this is not really a question

   you need to ask….but it is one I ask myself a lot during

   football season!)

Know what questions you should be asking

instinctively. And when a question pops into your mind and your

gut is telling you to ask it….ask it. You might be pleasantly

surprised at the answer!

$$$

Money Maker #14: It's All in the Details!

Those who succeed in recruiting – or any business for that matter - tend to pay attention to the details. They don't gloss over things and they don't cut corners. They know what is needed and how to get the job done. And they realize that in order to succeed and do their job well, they have to go way beneath the surface….they need to know and get into the details. If you pay attention to the details, you WILL make money. Both sides of this business – candidate and client – are very similar. They run parallel to each other and in most cases, we do the same things on both sides, all the while adjusting and conforming to the audience we are working with and speaking to. So where do details come in? Let's take a look….

The Candidate Side of our Business

I can't tell you how many times recruiters take resumes at face value and do not probe into the details of a candidate's background. If you have a form for information gathering during an interview with a candidate, use it. It is not a crutch. On the contrary, it demonstrates your professionalism and your interest in providing comprehensive service to the candidate. It helps capture all the details you will need to effectively control, manage and, most importantly, close a candidate. And, it also allows you to effectively communicate all this information to you teammates and clients. A resume by itself will not give this depth of information. Yet, I see it all the time….an email comes across the wire…."Hot candidate! Here's the resume" …then, the recruiters and account executives in the office begin to ask questions. How did they present? Have you checked references? Did you GET references? Why did they leave their last job…and the job before that….and the job before that? How did they get their current job? What is their reason for leaving? What's their current compensation? Do they get any bonus? Is it realized? When is it paid out? When was their last increase? How big is their company? Their department? What software do they know and are comfortable with? Are they active on the market? Did you discuss a counter offer with them? How much notice will they need to give? What are their top 3 criteria for their next opportunity...besides more money and a shorter commute? What's the sizzle on this candidate – what have they made, saved, or achieved at their current employer? ....you get my point. Unfortunately, when questions start flying, the recruiter representing that candidate tends to get defensive, irate and simply demands that the candidate be presented to the client. Personally, I don't present those candidates. You want my time? You need to give me details. And it has to be in the database so I can refer to it without bothering you and taking up your time. As a client, if I ask these questions and the recruiter does not have a sizeable majority of the answers, my confidence in that recruiter is shot.

The Client Side of our Business

I can't tell you how many times emailed job descriptions are STILL accepted as a job order. A job description is NOT a job order. Again, you should have a job order intake form on hand to ensure critical and comprehensive information is gathered when taking a job order. Use a form. It helps capture all the details we need to work a job order and, more importantly, to communicate to your team exactly what is expected from the client. A job description alone will not give you this. Yet, I see it all the time….an email comes across the wire…. "Hot job! Here's the description." Then, the recruiters start to ask questions… "What's the culture like? What's the manager's background? What's the sizzle – how do we 'sell' the company? How big is the team? Why is the position open? Is there a bonus? What is it, how is it calculated, and historically, has it been paid out? How long has the position been open? Have they seen any candidates or made any offers? Why/why not? What have they liked/disliked in the candidates they have seen thus far? What software do they use?" …..you get my point. Unfortunately, when the questions start flying, if the recruiter or account executive who wrote the "job order" does not have answers, they tend to get defensive, irate and simply demand that recruiters find and present candidates based on the job description. Personally, I don't work on those orders. You want my time? You need to give me details. And it has to be in the database so I can refer to it without bothering you and taking up your time. If we do not provide details on a job, how can we expect recruiters to recruit talent for that job? And if candidates ask these questions and the recruiter does not have a sizeable majority of the answers, they lose confidence in that recruiter.

Detailed information allows you to identify the right solution. For example….if a football coach is preparing for a game and is talking to his quarterback about an opposing defense they will be facing, he could say, "Watch out, they will blitz a lot." While that is good information, it is very superficial. Now, a better, more prepared coach says something like, "Watch out, they blitz a lot. They tend to taunt you with the weak-side linebacker and then send the strong-side linebacker and the safety on a blitz. Their D-line runs a lot of stunts and tends to shift position often prior to the snap to try to confuse you, and when they bring 7 men in the box, 90% of the time, it's a scare tactic and they end up dropping back into a zone coverage." Clearly, having more details will enable that quarterback to be more prepared to deliver solutions against that defense. In our business, you are the coach…and the quarterback! It is up to you to get whatever information you need to best handle and work a situation.

There are many, many more instances where details make all the difference. The key is to dive into the details and get that information. Peel back the layers – don't just be an order taker, so to speak. We need information to do our jobs and we will never get the necessary level of information we need if we do not ask for it….and ask for it…..and ask for it. Ask, ask, ask….probe, probe, probe….stretch, stretch, stretch….test, test, test…..confirm, confirm, confirm.

Where and how do we make money? It's all in the details!

$$$

Money Maker #15: Perception is Reality!

Perception is reality. When you take a step back and think about this, this is a powerful statement. When you apply it, it is even more powerful. People believe what they see and hear (just look at the political scene for an example of this….talk about spinning perception!....but I digress). Because of this, how we conduct ourselves and our business is critically important. For the sake of keeping things simple, I will focus on a few key areas where perception can make or break you:

1) On the phone

Regardless what kind of day you are having, how tired you may be, how stressed you may be, the car accident you had on the way into work, the coffee you spilled on your desk….whatever the case may be….when you are speaking with someone from the outside, candidate or client, everything is great. Business is great (and it really is!). You and your team are extremely busy. The best people in the business community want to be associated with the best recruiters, and the best recruiters are those who are successful and who have busy desks. So, regardless if that is the current case or not, you have to give the *perception* that it is. I hate hearing a recruiter, when asked how business is going, say, "Pretty good….it's picking up…." Ugh! If you're on the other end of that phone, wouldn't you rather hear, "Great! We are extremely busy. The market is very strong right now." You want to be perceived as a leader in your market with a busy desk and numerous clients with numerous jobs they are paying you to fill. You want to be perceived as a leader in your market with a deep, talented candidate network that dwarfs your competition.

2) In-person meetings

Be it a client or candidate meeting, you only get once chance to make an impression. Be positive. Be confident. Remove the words "I think" from your vocabulary. You don't think, you know. Dress to impress. Be well groomed. Be organized, researched and prepared. Be structured. Have an agenda. Ask probing questions. Listen. Listen. Listen. At the end of your meeting, you want the other person left with the perception that they are talking with the right person….that they made a good decision to work with you….the perception that they are in good hands.

3) On the Internet

I don't think I need to remind everyone of the dangers of social networking sites and the fact that photos and words put out there can and will come back to haunt you. Don't ever post something on a site or send something in an email that you would not want published for the world to see. Period. Of more direct relevance to this topic are job advertisement postings. Most companies invest thousands and thousands of dollars in subscriptions to online job boards. They have technology that sends ads across the Internet to numerous sites. If you work at such an organization, you should be taking full advantage of this luxury. Just as important as the candidate networking opportunities your ads yield (I know that clients want the passive candidates…I don't disagree…but it is the *active candidates* who give us market knowledge, leads, referrals, etc. and cannot be ignored) and the market presence ads deliver. Decades ago it was the newspapers. You ran ads not just to get candidates, but also to show a presence, to give the perception in the market that you had the best and most job opportunities. That you were *busy*. Today, that perception has to be delivered via the Internet. If you go to a market and run a job board search, the firm that shows up with the most great-sounding job postings gives the perception that they are busy! So....first of all, post your jobs! Second, do more than just post a job description. Remember the sizzle! Tell candidates why they would want to work for this company. Give them a compelling reason to want to send you a resume or reach out and talk to you. Cast the net wide....even candidates who don't meet all the technical criteria may be someone you want to know (and who probably know other people!!!). Craft your ads....put a little zip in them.

Perception is reality. What perception are you giving in your local market?

$$$

Money Maker #16: Prepping...the Candidate AND the Client!

Prior Preparation Prevents Poor Performance. These are the essential "5 P's" of life. We should apply it to ourselves, yes, and should be passing this onto our candidates and clients prior to every meeting that takes place between a candidate and a client. In the world of recruiting, it's all about control. There are many things we can do to improve and maximize our ability to control the placement cycle. One of those "things" is preparing (prepping) the candidate and client prior to their meeting each other. Here's the good news: Most of your competition (not all, but most) does a horrible job in this area. They provide only surface level information to the candidate (company name, who to ask for, maybe a job description) and send the person out to do what they may. The client? Most don't even bother prepping the client. They just look for the follow-up call after the meeting....and wait.....and wait. Promise yourself that this will never be you. Promise yourself that you will never have a client/candidate meeting take place without all parties being as prepared as they can be. It is *your* responsibility as a recruiter to ensure this happens. Your candidates and clients will appreciate it and you will make a very positive impression on them in the process….and you will differentiate yourself from your competition. All good things!

For the candidate:

I always recommend scheduling the prep call the evening before the day of the interview (or meeting). I suggest this simply because if you call during the day when they are at work, their attention is not 100% on you, and they will more than likely not be able to talk freely. Secondly, you want to talk with them the night before so that all the infinite wisdom you bestow upon them is fresh in their mind the next day. Make the prep a planned, scheduled calendar event with the candidate so they realize the importance of the call. This is not a short call nor should it be a rushed call. A strong prep can easily last 20 – 30 minutes. A few tips for a strong candidate prep call:

- **Make it Interactive**. Don't spend the entire call talking *"to"* your candidate….get them involved. It should be a two-way, interactive discussion.

- **Role play**. Ask your candidate questions – especially the "classic" ones you know will be asked in an interview – and see how they respond. This will allow you to provide better feedback and coaching depending on how good (or bad) their responses are.

- **Provide and discuss information that is specific to the hiring managers**. If the job order is not yours, involve your teammate and do this together with the candidate. Personality traits, background, management style, idiosyncrasies, etc….all good things for your candidate to know before going in.

- **Review things of particular importance as related to the specific job/position**. If your candidate has experience in an area that is critically important to the hiring manager's needs, be sure they know to make sure that experience is discussed.

- **Proactively deal with potential areas of concern** (job history, gaps, etc.) that you know the client will want to discuss. Make sure your candidate is prepared to handle these "sensitive" topics that can often be deal killers.

- **Coach them on how to close out the interview strongly**. Make sure they express interest in the opportunity, ask about concerns, and inquire about next steps.

- Make sure the candidate knows to **call you as soon as they are done** with the interview. Immediately. Make sure they understand that this is for their benefit so that you can be prepared to go to work for them when you speak with the hiring manager.

- **Re-close** (because this should not be the first time you are doing so) the candidate on money, counter offer, notice and other opportunities that may be in play.

- **Don't forget the "little" things** like making sure the candidate knows where they are going and what they should wear (especially for more junior candidates). I know most of us think this is a given but you'd be surprised.

- **Repeat prior to every interview** in the cycle….not just the first one. Let the candidate know you will be doing this, and that it may be repetitive but it is your job to make sure they are as prepared as they can be prior to any interview.

For the client:

We often forget about prepping on this side of the deal, and it is just as important to do so. Be sure to have a discussion with your client prior to any meeting or interview they may have with a candidate. A few tips for a strong client prep call:

- **Review why the candidate is good for the opportunity**. Re-highlight specific skills that are important to the client based on initial discussions about the need.

- **Discuss items of importance for your candidate** that the client should discuss during the send out. If your candidate needs to hear certain things from your client, let them know this. Hearing "sells" from a recruiter is one thing, but hearing the same "sells" from the hiring manager has a greater impact and can make or break a deal.

- **Re-close** on compensation/budget needs, timeline for hire and process/next steps. Be proactive and try to stay a step or two ahead of your client. Guide and lead them.

- **Review and discuss any other candidates they may have interviewed for the same position**, what they've liked, not liked and how many are still in consideration.

- Remind them you will want to speak with them **immediately** after the send out to get their feedback and to make sure we keep the candidate focused on their opportunity and the process moving since it is a very competitive climate for top talent.

- **Repeat prior to every meeting/interview** in the cycle…not just the first one.

$$$

There is obviously much more that goes into making strong prep calls. Develop your own style and figure out what works for you. Above all, never have a send out take place without conducting strong prep calls with your client and candidate. It is yet another way to maintain control of the process.

Maximize your chances for success. Prep all parties involved prior to a client/candidate interview....EVERY interview!

$$$

Money Maker #17: The Client Visit

Client Visits. Recruiters love them….recruiters need them….recruiters are able to identify talent much more efficiently and effectively after one has taken place. There are so many benefits of a client visit – too numerous to mention – yet we often start working job orders without ever spending face time with the hiring manager. If you are a long-lines recruiter, an "in-person" client visit is often not an option. In those cases, it has to be a virtual visit. The premise is still the same: Get to know your client as well as you can, and you will be in a much better position to know what kind of candidate they look for when they do hire. Any candidate we present to a client should be technically qualified to do the job. It usually comes down to which candidate will mesh best within the client environment, and we cannot get that from a job description.

Whether you have a job order or not, a recruiter should always strive to get a meeting with a hiring manager. Some in the industry would disagree with me on this point, arguing that recruiters should only meet with clients who are prepared to give them business right now. I disagree. Ours is a relationship business. If we foster relationships early, we are that much more ahead of the game once business does come in. When scheduling and conducting client visits, my advice to you is **PACK** your bags!

Prepare

Always remember the 5 "Ps." Prior Preparation Prevents Poor Performance. Know it....live it....commit to it. Research the company...company website, news releases, Google searches, Hoovers, etc. Research the hiring manger(s)....LinkedIn, company website bios, etc. Research job openings....search job boards and website careers pages for current and past listings. Identify trends. Bring two copies of a business agreement with you to the meeting. If there is a job order to work, you are then positioned to negotiate terms and, if need be, line out and initialize changes to the forms. You and the manager can then sign them and be off and running. This saves time. Have an agenda and know your objective(s) of the meeting.

ASK

Be respectful of the hiring manager's time. Acknowledge on the front end and stick to the agreed duration. Ask questions - a lot of them. Have a prepared list with you to maximize your time. Use a job order form or some sort of prompter if available so you will not forget to ask and obtain information you are seeking. As points are brought up, echo them back to ensure an understanding has been reached and that you are in sync with what the hiring manager is saying. Praise any successes within the company or the manager's group that are known or that come up in conversation.

Develop the "unique hiring profile" that manager looks for when hiring. Obtain "sizzle" about the company, department, manager, etc. that will help you sell the company to potential candidates. Map out an org chart, across the company and within the manager's group. Find out who their main competitors are. Ask how they are performing against their business plan. Get information on the company's benefits.

Ask for referrals within the company - who else should you be reaching out to that could benefit from your services? Ask them what they expect from you? What has their experience with recruiters been? Where/how have they used recruiters? Are they able to use them now if the situation merits it?

CLOSE

Close to some sort of future action - from a follow-up call to a candidate interview - whatever it may be. Make sure you close to *something* before you leave the meeting. If there is business to be had, close by asking for the business. Be aggressive, enthusiastic and proactive.

KNOW

When you leave, you should have a clear understanding of the company, the manager and any potential opportunities you may have for business with them. If, in the future, someone asks you a question about the company or hiring manager, be it a teammate or a candidate, you should have most of the answers.

Qualify the account. Determine if it is worth your time and effort to pursue and market to them, if it is worth it but just not immediately, or if the company is not worth your time at all. Be sure to document the information you obtained in a database for future use by you and your teammates.

Obviously there's more information to garner. The key is, when we have the opportunity to get in front of a prospect or client, we need to seize that moment. When we have a job order, we tend to ask a lot of detailed questions. When we do not, we tend to stay "on the surface". I would encourage you to always ask as many detailed questions as possible so that, when the opportunity arises and you are ready to get to work, you don't have to spend/waste time with questions you could have already asked. When you have the opportunity to work a job order, your candidates and teammates will have questions. The more answers you have readily available at your fingertips, the more credibility you will earn.

Meet your clients. It sounds basic and simple enough. It sounds like a given. If we are going to work with and for an organization to help them secure talent, it makes logical sense that we would initially spend some time with them. Unless you are a long-lines recruiter and do all of your work over the phone, there is no reason why you should work a job order for a client without having met them (at least in my mind…call me crazy). Even worse, why would you work a job order for a client who flat-out refuses to allocate the time to meet with you – the person they expect to deliver talent? Clients who will not meet with you clearly do not value or respect you or what you do (at least in my mind…call me crazy). Not meeting your client before working an order?

Let's see…..if I take a job order and I never meet the client I am working for….and all they do is send me a job description and ask me for resumes….who's in control here? Not me! I would not consider *that* a client at all. As a matter of fact, I wouldn't even consider that a job order. And if I do decide to work that order, how can I honestly expect my teammates to help me recruit for it? Conversations would go something like this:

"What's the hiring manager like?"

"uh….I dunno. Didn't meet them."

"What's the environment like?"

"uh….I dunno. Didn't go there. They're *real* busy right now. But, hey – they're a *really* good company and this is a *really* good opportunity and they are *really* ready to hire."

….yeah. Right. If I am "that" recruiter, I sound like a fool (at least in my mind….call me crazy).

Meet your clients. Meet any and all decision makers that will have a say in the process. At a minimum, at least meet THE decision maker. It's how the best in the business do business. It's about setting that whole "client/recruiter relationship" expectation. Hold yourself – and your clients – to a higher standard. I don't care if the job order was passed to you by one of your teammates who just visited with that client. YOU need to meet with them because now it's YOUR job order! YOU now stand to make a considerable amount of money should it get filled, so YOU have to own it.

$$$

At the core, recruiting is a simple business. Unfortunately we, as recruiters, often make it harder than it has to be. When we do not meet our clients, we make our job harder.

Too often, I am hearing that recruiters are working job orders where they have not met the client…and they've never been to the facility…and that the client is too busy to meet them and just wants resumes….and all we have to go on is a job description. That is a crappy way to do business. You are better than that.

Meet your clients…. and expect your teammates to do the same. Hold yourself and your peers accountable to do so.

Money Maker #18: ABC….Always Be Closing!

ABC – "Always Be Closing." It is every salesperson's credo. They are words to live by. While we often say it, we do not always do it. When it is offer time, we always hunker down and get into closing mode. We strategize, look at every angle, prepare for objections, etc. The thing is, if we start to close at the offer stage, we're too late. There are numerous times during a candidate placement lifecycle where we need to be closing – both candidate and client – in order to maximize our chances for success and remain in control of the situation.

Closing should not be an event. It should be part of the entire process and something that, instinctively, you are always doing. Closing starts at the initial meeting, be it the candidate interview or client meeting. These are critical opportunities when we have to ask questions, gather information, and gain a thorough understanding of what a candidate or client needs. There are some fantastic prompters/forms that guide you in your questioning and ensure that no stone is left unturned, and I highly recommend using them in such a manner. I have included some in the back of this book for your reference.

On the candidate side, we need to know *specifically* why they would leave their current employer for another (the candidate's "pushes"). We need to know *specifically* what they need to see in another opportunity for it to make sense for them – what their top 3 criteria are….and what they mean to that candidate….and why they are important to them (the candidate's "pulls"). We need them to break down what they need us to deliver, so that when we do, there is no question we have done our job. On the client side, we need to take a *complete* job order, not just get a copy of a job description and a salary range. We have to get them to break down what kind of profile they need us to deliver, so that when we do, there is no question we have done our job. All of this, ideally, should be done in person. If we do this, the basis of our close throughout the rest of the placement process is the candidate's / client's own words. Why "sell" when you can simply echo a person's own words that they told you to begin with? The key is to remember to get that information up front.

From that point on, with every conversation you have with that candidate or client, you should always be reconfirming that basic information, uncovering any new information, and planning for future events. Times we should remember to close (after the initial meeting) include:

- The matching call (when you are calling a candidate to 'pitch' them an opportunity)

- The prep call (prior to any client/candidate interview. EVERY prep call – candidate and client)

- The debrief call (after any client/candidate interview. EVERY debrief call – candidate and client)

- The offer stage (ALWAYS trial close before actually extending an offer. Even if you have the offer in hand)

- The acceptance stage

- The resignation stage

- During a candidate's 2-week notice transition period (because we all know that counter offers can and will happen at any time during this period)

At each of these stages, we need to constantly be verifying and closing on current compensation, needed compensation (what number the candidate is *truly* deliverable at), counter offer, notice, start date and more. Do not assume anything, because we all know that when you assume, you make an…..well, you know. If we do our job right, and take the time to gather the appropriate information up front, deals should close themselves…..*should*. If we do our job right, we should never have to 'sell' anything. When we end up selling, we have not done our job well enough up front.

When initially interviewing a new candidate, it helps to have some sort of prompter or outline to guide you through that meeting. Doing so ensures that you will not forget to obtain critical information that you will need to effectively represent, manage, and close that candidate throughout a placement cycle. Here is one example of a candidate interview outline:

✓ Start with a simple agenda:

- I want to tell you a little about me and my company.

- I then want to learn about you, your background and what types of opportunities might be of interest to you going forward.

- Finally, we'll discuss how we are going to work together.

✓ What is your current situation / what are the main reasons you are looking to make a move?

✓ What, ideally, would you be looking for in your next opportunity? If you could write your own job description what would it look like?

✓ What are your professional strengths? If I was starting accompany and asked you to come work with me, where could you add immediate value?

✓ When you evaluate an opportunity, excluding money and commute, what are your top 3 criteria that have to be there in order for the opportunity to make sense for you?

For each criterion the candidate mentions, ask these two follow-up questions to gain a deeper understanding:

What does that mean to you?

Why is that important?

✓ Next, go through their job history, the last 10 years of their career, from past to present. For each employer, find out starting and ending salary (including bonuses, etc.), how they found the opportunity and reasons for leaving, ending with their current compensation.

✓ Find out when they last received an increase in base salary.

✓ Ask about their current benefits, including medical/dental/vision (and how much they currently pay for it), if they cover themselves or others as well on their benefits, how much vacation they currently receive, is there a 401(k)? Is there a match? Any other perks?

✓ Inquire about commute threshold – how long they can bear commuting one way to work. Also inquire if they are open to relocation. If so, what areas are of interest?

- ✓ Ask if they are actively sending out resumes and/or interviewing for opportunities. If so, inquire as to what kind of opportunities they are targeting. Also ask if their resume is posted on any job boards.

- ✓ Inquire about their availability to interview – if one of your clients is interested in meeting with them, how much lead time do they need to make arrangements in their schedule?

- ✓ Obtain professional references.

- ✓ If they are currently employed, discuss counter offer.

- ✓ Close with a strong wrap-up, explaining how we are going to work together and all we potentially could do for them.

- ✓ Source for other positions/profiles.

Our product is a living human being, not an inanimate object and, well, sometimes life happens and there are things that derail a placement that we simply cannot control. While that is true, there is plenty that we can control. And like Janet Jackson once said, "It's all about control!" Close early. Close often. Always Be Closing!

$$$

Money Maker #19: It's All About Compromise!

Compromise is the key to many things in business and in life. It is a necessity in every deal that is made. We compromise with candidates when scheduling interviews in order to work around their schedule. We compromise with clients when negotiating fees. Clients compromise on their candidate skill requirements. Candidates compromise on their commute threshold. Compromise a key in forging lasting relationship – both personally and professionally (take it from one who has been married for more than 25 years....trust me....a LOT of compromising has gone on in that relationship...but I digress).

Compromise is a give and take. You always have to be willing to give a little in order to expect something from the other side. You never want to be the one who is always giving and not getting anything in return (or vice versa, for that matter). That is not compromise. That is taking advantage of someone or of a situation. Eventually, that will come back to haunt you in some way, shape or form. To compromise, you need to communicate. You need to have and be able to process information. You need to know what your goals and limitations are, what you are willing to part with, and what you expect in return. If a client wants a reduced fee, for example, they should be willing to give up something....commit to an exclusive, a reduced guarantee....get something in return. Don't be the recruiter in the following scenario:

Recruiter: Our fee is 30%.

Client: We do business at 20%.

Recruiter: Ok. Our payment terms are net 10.

Client: Our payment terms need to be 90 days.

Recruiter: Ok. We offer a 30-day replacement guarantee.

Client: We expect a 30-day money back guarantee.

Recruiter: Ok. When you interview our candidates, I will need detailed feedback.

Client: I will never call you back. Any questions?

Recruiter: Uh....well, what do I get in return for all this?

Client: You get my business.

Recruiter: Oh. Ok.

$$$

Too often recruiters feel the need to give, give, and give in order to get job orders. That is no way to start or grow a good client relationship. Be honest with your client and yourself. Each party should be willing to compromise when and where appropriate. By doing so and by standing up for yourself in compromising situations, you will earn more respect from those around you, including your clients, and be better off for it. Don't be afraid to walk away from business that does not make sense, and don't be afraid to walk away from clients and candidates who are not willing to compromise. Remember, you control where you spend your time. Don't EVER compromise on that!

"Are we negotiating? …..Always!"
(Taken from a dialogue between Al Pacino and Keanu Reeves in the motion picture, *The Devil's Advocate)*

"We don't take NO for an answer!"
"Let's show this client who's boss!"

100

"Bleed 'em for all they're worth!"

…while these are some phrases one might hear in preparing for a negotiation, they do not represent what a *good* negotiator's mindset should be. As recruiters, we are constantly in negotiating mode. Negotiating fees, start dates, guarantee periods, splits….it is a daily function of our job. While we always want to be in control of a negotiation, how can we position ourselves to do that? Let's recall a fundamental principle of recruiting (and life): The only two things we have control over are **time** and **information**. That being said, we should spend some **time** gathering **information** prior to entering into a negotiation with another party. How many of us do this? No…really.

Most of the time, we are moving at light speed and "don't have time" to prepare for much of anything. We head out to a client visit, take a job order, and all of a sudden we are negotiating fees, terms, requirements, etc. without any prior preparation. Most of the time, that negotiation begins without either party knowing what is important or what the other is hoping to gain. To paraphrase from a book I recently read, negotiations should always be WIN-win. Both parties should win….but you should win more! Remember this: A truly successful negotiation takes place when all partied involved walk away feeling like they have won. If any of the parties walks away feeling cheated or taken advantage of, it is a failed negotiation. Think of how many times we approach a new client/prospect, and they want us to abide by their terms….all of them….not willing to negotiate or flex on anything.

Recruiter: "Our terms are 30%, 30 day replacement and net 10 payment terms."

Client: "We'll do business at 20%, 90 day money back, 30 day payment terms."

Recruiter: "Is any part of that negotiable?"

Client: "No."

Recruiter: "All righty then!"

Wow….that's some negotiating, huh? Hardly! Negotiations are not always smooth. They can and will hit roadblocks. Talks will stall. And this is all very much ok. Some negotiations are easy and others take time. It is better to work through it and arrive at a mutually agreed upon deal than to rush into a bad one for the sake of getting it done. Prior to a negotiation, do some research. Get to know your audience, their background, their company. Get information on prior deals they have been involved in. Try to learn their habits, their strengths, their weaknesses, and what is important to them. Prior to entering into a negotiation, know *your* goals and objectives and also know your limits – your bottom line. What are you willing to part with or bend on in exchange for getting something you desire? During negotiations, whenever you sense a reservation, probe. Ask questions. Gather information. Get to the root of the reservation and figure out what it is the other party is looking for and what the true barrier is in the negotiation. Then and only then can you work on getting creative enough to arrive at a solution that benefits all. Again, the key is making sure the other party walks away feeling satisfied with the deal. If they achieve their goal and you achieve yours, it's all good!

$$$

Negotiation is an art. It is a skill. And like any skill, it gets better with practice. So, it's ok to not take "NO" for an answer, to "show the client who's boss" and to "bleed 'em for all their worth" ....as long as the client walks away from the negotiating table happy! That is the key. Both parties need to be content with the negotiations that took place. Remember, if you are going to 'give' during a negotiation, always try and 'get' something in return. One side should not be doing all the giving or all the getting. For example, if you grant your client a longer guarantee period or extend the payment terms, get a higher fee, pre-scheduled interview time slots, or some level of exclusivity in return. If you are going to discount your fee, try to gain commitment for a Company In (see Money Maker #20). Typically, most recruiters have some degree of flexibility in terms of fee percentage, guarantee period, and payment terms. Use those areas to your advantage. And remember to not discount your fee for 'perceived' volume business (i.e. "we are planning to hire a lot more in the future"). Make sure the volume is real and guaranteed.

$$$

Money Maker #20: Close More Deals More Often:

The Company In!

Wouldn't it be great if you could decide who your clients

interview, when they interview them, and in what order they are

interviewed? You can....we just don't think of doing it often

enough. As recruiters, we always want to have as much control over

a placement cycle as possible, and there is no greater level of control

than through the **Company In** – a process by which you invite your

client into your office to meet several qualified, pre-screened

candidates in a back-to-back format. This process affords you the

opportunity to bring *your* client into *your* office to interview *your*

candidates in the order that *you* decide. That's got a very nice ring

to it, eh? Lots of control! You're leading the way and guiding your

client. Most recruiting firms have this process. Most recruiters,

however, do not utilize it. I've been with three national recruiting

firms during my career and I've always done these. Each firm

usually has a unique name for their version of this process, but the

name does not matter, it's the process that's key. Your client doesn't care what you call it, they care if you can deliver. And the Company In delivers....better than any other hiring process. Period. It's good for the client, it's good for the candidate and it's great for the recruiter. Deals can close within one week.

So, here's a quick review of some key points we need to know and remember:

- When you are meeting with a client, present the Company In as your standard mode of operation....as far as your client is concerned, it is how you do business. You are the expert. They need to trust you.

- Describe the process with confidence. Illustrate the value it brings to the client - there are many benefits including:

  o Saves time. Hires can happen in one week or less, and in about 5 hours of a client's time (as compared to a minimum of 3 weeks and about 15 hours through conventional means).

  o Less distraction, more focus. The client is out of their environment, so there are no interruptions or distractions. They can concentrate on the matter at hand – interviewing.

- o Higher success rate. On average, there is an 80% (or better) chance the client will be able to land the candidate of their choice out of the first group interviewed (vs. 20% through conventional means). This is because the process moves faster and reduces the possibility of candidates being wooed by other opportunities while interviewing for theirs.

- o Confidentiality. Since the interviews are conducted at your office, there is no risk of other employees at the client company wondering what the manager is interviewing for. This is especially beneficial when clients need to conduct confidential searches.

- In a Company In, the client interviews several qualified candidates in a back-to-back format in your office. In a "true" Company In, the client does not see or screen resumes prior to the interview day. They interview the candidates you choose to put in front of them. Remember, you are the expert. They need to trust you.

- When scheduling the interviews, put your strongest candidate (or at least the one you believe your client will like the most) in the 3rd time slot. The 3rd candidate to interview with your client will be the most prepared since you will have debrief notes from the first candidate to share with the third prior to that candidate meeting with the client.

- Set the expectation that the entire process is designed to be completed within one business week. Company In Monday, second interviews Wednesday or Thursday (at the client's office), offer and acceptance Friday. Done. Closed. Filled.

If every recruiter within a branch conducted one – just one – Company In per week, think of how many more deals your team would close each month (cha-CHING!). If a client needs to conduct a confidential search, needs to fill a position ASAP, or needs to hire multiple employees with the same profile, the Company In is a no-brainer. Whatever the case, have confidence in yourself and your team that you will be able to deliver. When a client interviews

candidates through a Company In, they will want to do it again and

again....and you will too!

$$$

Money Maker #21: Always Acknowledge and Clarify Before You Try To Solve an Objection!

In football, coaches prepare for their opponent by drafting a game plan. The offensive and defensive coordinators prepare schemes and specific plays based on what they expect to see from the opponent. Sometimes it works to perfection. More often than not, however, there comes a time in the game where the plan just stops working. They encounter a roadblock - an objection to their plan. When that happens, coaches need to adapt. They need to find a solution to the problem. First, however, they need to acknowledge the objection or situation - the problem that is preventing their team from accomplishing their goal. Once they acknowledge it, they can try to solve the problem, all the while keeping the initial objective in mind. Those who can do this effectively end up emerging victorious. If a coach starts off with a game plan heavily weighted on running the football, and the defense is showing strong resistance to the run, the coach cannot keep using the same plays over and over again hoping the resistance will stop. He has to acknowledge that the run is not working and call more passing plays to try to build success for his team while he figures out how to establish the run. He does not have to abandon the initial plan altogether, but he does have to adapt to the situation. Dome teams cannot run OR pass very well, so it doesn't really matter...but I digress.

The world of recruiting has similarities to the football game planning example. We enter into every phone call and every meeting with a plan. Sometimes that plan works to perfection, and we achieve our goal. More than not, however, we encounter resistance that forces us to adjust. The key is, we need to remember to acknowledge that resistance before we try to overcome it. Little phrases such as, "I understand" and "I can appreciate that" and "I'd be happy to do that" can put the other person at ease while you try to address and overcome their objection. They key is to actually *acknowledge* their objection or concern *first* before doing so. Don't discount or ignore their concern and push forward. That will only alienate them and give them the perception that you are not listening to them and don't care.

$$$

Consider the following recruiting and marketing call examples:

Example #1:

Recruiter: If there was an opportunity in the market that was far superior to your current situation would you want to hear about it?

Candidate: Absolutely.

Recruiter: What are you looking for?

Candidate: Whatcha got?

Recruiter: Well, first we have to meet.

Candidate: Tell me whatcha got?

Recruiter: Are you available this week to come into my office?

Candidate: I'd like to hear whatcha got?

Recruiter: If you're not willing to meet with me maybe you're not serious about exploring opportunities.

Candidate: I just want to know whatcha got?

…..clearly, this recruiter is NOT listening.

Example #2:

Recruiter: If there was an opportunity in the market that was far superior to your current situation would you want to hear about it?

Candidate: Absolutely.

Recruiter: What are you looking for?

Candidate: Whatcha got?

Recruiter: I'd be happy to share with you the opportunities that attracted me to your background. Before doing so, however, I would like to learn more about you and what is important to you so that I can be sure I present the right opportunity to you and not waste your time.

Candidate: Ok.

…..this recruiter listened, acknowledged that the "Whatcha Got" roadblock by simply telling the candidate they'd be happy to share details with them and then went back to the initial game plan by going for an in-person meeting to learn more about the candidate.

Example #3:

Client: Send me the resume

Recruiter: Tell me about the job.

Client: Send me the resume.

Recruiter: What skills are important.

Client: *click*

Example #4

Client: Send me the resume.

Recruiter: I'd be happy to send you the resume. First, if I may, I'd like to ask a few questions about what you would be looking for in an employee so that I do not waste your time by sending over a candidate that would not be in line with your needs.

….again, the "I'd be happy to" acknowledges the roadblock, puts the client at ease knowing that the recruiter actually listened and heard them, and allows the recruiter to continue on. It mitigates the situation a bit.

Recruiters, like all sales professionals, are conditioned to expect objections. We train on how to handle and overcome objections all the time. The key is to be disciplined enough to first *acknowledge* the objection and *clarify* what it is before trying to overcome it. We have to convey the perception that we hear the other party, appreciate their position, and want to work with them. Then we need to continue with our plan and gather more information so we can modify our game plan and achieve our goal. And if that doesn't work, just punt! (only kidding)

People want to be heard. That's not too much to ask, is it? Unfortunately, many in our profession do just the opposite. Recruiters are always selling, always talking, and unfortunately not listening nearly enough. When people feel ignored, they lose trust. When they lose trust, we lose control. When they feel heard…when they feel acknowledged…they begin to trust. When we have trust, we get control.

$$$

We talk to people all day every day. And in many
conversations, we are faced with objections. We hear them all the
time. From candidates and from clients. They are part of our
everyday lives as recruiters. We need to overcome them....or do
we? Think about it. When someone has an objection to something,
what are they looking for from the other person they are talking
with? Usually, they are simply looking to be heard, looking to be
understood, or looking for empathy. In most cases, our candidates
and clients are no different. So, when faced with an objection, the
first thing you should do is **Acknowledge** that objection. It is a
simple act that speaks volumes and it can bring down defense walls,
allowing you to continue your conversation. If you fail to
acknowledge the objection, you run the risk of alienating your
audience and losing trust. Once you have acknowledged the
objection, you then simply table it....set it aside, so to speak...and
redirect the conversation. But you first have to acknowledge the
objection so that the person feels like they have been heard.
Some examples of this technique:

$$$

Example 1: Avoidance

Candidate: "How much does the job pay?"

Recruiter: "I can't discuss that with you – it's confidential."

Example 2: Acknowledgment

Candidate: "How much does the job pay?"

Recruiter: "I'd be happy to discuss compensation with you. What are you currently earning?"

Example 3: Avoidance

Client: "Send me the resume."

Recruiter: "I can't do that until we have a business agreement in place."

Example 4: Acknowledgement

Client: "Send me the resume."

Recruiter: "I'd be happy to send you the resume. Could you please tell me a little more about what type of person you are looking to hire?"

$$$

Acknowledge – Table – Redirect. By using this technique,

you will extend your conversations. And when we extend

conversations, good things begin to happen!

$$$

Money Maker #22: Tailor That Resume!

The resume. It represents you....and for recruiters, it represents the candidate, you, and the firm you work for. For all of those reasons, we need to take a hard look at a candidate's resume before showing it to a client. Our "do it now" mentality and high sense of urgency sometimes gets in the way and we end up sending the client a resume that is not strong enough, doesn't represent the candidate's abilities as well as it could, or just plain looks bad. We need to own the process. We need to control the process. And part of that involves taking responsibility for making sure that a candidate's resume is as strong as it can be before presenting it to a hiring manager for consideration. We always tell candidates they should do this when applying for jobs on their own, so why shouldn't we? We should!

In our world, as much as we would rather not have to show them, clients often demand to see the resumes of candidates we want them to interview. Those resumes had better be impressive and tailored to the job. Every job is different and every hiring manager

$$$

has their own unique hiring profile – things they look for – in

addition to specific skills and abilities needed to perform specific

jobs. Your candidate's resume should reflect those things that are

applicable to the job. As a result, it is not uncommon that we will

have different versions of a candidate's resume being sent out to

different hiring managers based on what that manager's specific hot

buttons are. And again, this is *our* responsibility as the recruiter, not

the candidate's. Throughout my entire career in recruiting, I have

never – not once – presented a resume to a client without modifying

it or enhancing it in some way. Sometimes resumes ~~would~~ require

total makeovers. For some passive candidates, a resume did not

exist and had to be written. In any case, be it making enhancements

to a resume, inserting more "sizzle" and details that you know your

hiring manager is looking to see, or doing a complete re-write, we

need to own that process. *We* need to be doing that. Remember, it's

all about control. If we assign that job to the candidate, we lose

control, we lose time, we lose momentum….we lose. All too often I

hear, "I have a great candidate….I'm just waiting for them to update their resume and get it back to me, and then I will present it to the client." When this happens, you lose control. You are totally dependent on that candidate's ability to perform the work needed and get it back to you…on their time table. I could never do that. I don't like giving up control over something that I can control myself. Plus, if the candidate was unable to write an acceptable resume the first time around, how can we expect them to write a better one the second time? Think about that. We should work with the candidate to get this accomplished in an acceptable time frame, and *we* should drive this process. Set up a call or a meeting where you can talk with your candidate and pull information that you need to update the resume. Once you make the modifications, email the resume to the candidate and have them review it for accuracy and to ensure you have not overlooked any critical information. They should see what you are sending to your client (if for no other reason than the fact that when they meet with the client, you don't want them making the mistake of giving them their original resume….which will not look like the one you submitted….and then that causes a bunch of questions by the client, so be sure you do this). Once you have completed the enhancements and tailored the resume to the job you are submitting it for, you are ready to show it to your client.

You get one chance to make a first impression. For us, sometimes it is that first resume we submit to a new client. Is it strong enough? Does it contain the right information your client has told you is required for the position? Is it tailored to the job? If not, we make a horrible impression. Why take that chance? So, a few suggestions coming from someone who, throughout his entire recruiting career, has never, ever presented a resume to a client without tailoring, modifying, or reformatting it in some way.

- Tailor each resume to the job for which it is being presented. Expand on areas that will be of importance to your client and highlight/bold skills and experience that will mean the most to him/her. This, of course, requires that you have an in-depth knowledge of what your client wants. A resume is never a static document. It is not a one size fits all.

- Make sure the resume is content rich. Be sure it contains lots of MSA (Made, Saved and Achieved) information. Quantifiable accomplishments the candidate has attained. The resume should not simply state *what* a candidate has done; it should display *how* what that candidate has done has positively impacted their employers. Think numbers and percentages and be as specific as you can. That is what truly separates the strong from the weak.

- If modifications need to be made to a candidate's resume, you have one of two options: (a) let the candidate make them and send you the update or (b) extract the information needed and YOU make the modifications to the resume. I of course, being the control freak that I am, always chose option 'b' so I did not fall victim to a candidate's timetable. That being said, whenever you do make modifications, remember to send the finished product to the candidate for review to ensure you have accurately represented everything. Also, make sure when they get a send out, that they take YOUR revised version of the resume (the one your client will also have) to that meeting. Nothing is more embarrassing or deal-threatening than having a candidate present a resume to a client that is different from the one you sent them.

- Make it easy for your client to read. Keep it simple, use consistent verb tenses, and a font/pitch that is easy to read.

- Always use a chronological format as opposed to a functional one. Clients prefer it 99.99% of the time.

- Use action verbs. Every bullet-point/sentence under a candidate's experience should start with an action verb (managed, attained, supervised, created, deployed....). The resume should not read like a job description.

- Make sure there is no first- or third-person verbiage. John does not like that!

There is more – much more – that can be said on the topic of resume writing. The bottom line is, a candidate's resume represents them....and when we show it to a client, it represents us. And a

$$$

strong resume can make all the difference! With resumes, one size does not fit all. Be sure you are tailoring your candidate resumes before showing them to your clients.

$$$

Money Maker #23: Keep A Hot List!

Candidates. We meet them by the thousands. Some are good, some are bad, and some are walking placements. We call the latter candidates **HOT**!

These candidates – the hot candidates – should always be on the forefront of our minds....easily accessible and easy to remember. When someone walks into your office and shouts out a hot new job order, most recruiters will open their database and immediately conduct a search on their candidates. They will sift through them, line by line, name by name, opening up some, closing others....it can be time consuming and in our world, time is always of the essence. To speed up this process, keep a hot list of candidates. The key is to constantly update the list with current hot candidates that you know would make a move for the right opportunity. These candidates are not just "good "candidates. They are the best of the best you have. The *crème de la crème*. They are candidates that if put in front of a hiring manager, will get the job. They are true MPCs (Most Place-able Candidates). We know

126

what they want, we know what they offer, and we have a clear line of communication as to how we are going to work together.

If you are not already doing so, make a hot list. Use a white board, use Excel, use tools that your database offers, use a piece of paper.....I don't care how you do it, just do it! Each recruiter should have a hot list at their desks that is current and updated at all times. Some groups may choose to have a centralized white board where the entire team's hot candidates are listed...maybe with recruiter initials next to them to indicate ownership. Again, I don't care how you do it, just do it. Section the hot list by position title. Start with your demand area titles – those positions in the market that are typically always in demand (in accounting for example, this would be Staff Accountant, Senior Accountant and Financial Analyst) and then expand into other titles that come up (in accounting, I would recommend adding Accounting Manager, Controller, Cost Accountant, and yes, Audit and Tax.....those who know me know how much I just LOVE seeing recruiters work on Audit and Tax searches, but we do get them so we might as well keep track of the best candidates we have in those areas). You get the idea. My bet is that the most successful recruiters already do this. Learn from them. Keeping a hot list allows for a quick look to see if you have any candidates that are needed for job orders as they come in. It also allows you to quickly reference hot candidate profiles while on the phone with a client. Finally, it can also be a wakeup call to increase your candidate inventory. If you look at your hot list and there are only a few names on it, hit the recruiting trail and beef it up! Remember....you should always recruit for talent, not just for open job orders.

Keep a hot list. If you do, your client/candidate interview activity just might heat up!

Money Maker #24: Trial Close Your Candidates Before Extending an Offer!

You know what I absolutely hate hearing when I am in a branch? "We have an offer out to a candidate, and we are waiting to hear back from them." Ugh! We work way too hard to have deals fall apart at the offer stage, but they do. And when that does happen, sometimes...well, more often than not....well, most of the time....ok, almost always....it is our fault. As recruiters, when deals fall apart, 99.9% of the time it is due to recruiter error. Somewhere, somehow along the way we missed something. Maybe we never really closed our candidate on money. Maybe we never asked those tough questions to fish out possible deal breakers. Maybe we didn't do a good job of actually interviewing the candidate. And maybe we didn't trial close before we extended the offer. That last one is sooooooo crucial.

We get paid to deliver candidates to clients. Not to recruit them, not to screen them, not to present them....to deliver them. When a client makes their selection and makes your candidate an offer, you want them to accept it. On the spot. Without hesitation. We don't get offers so that our candidates can think about it. When it comes time to extend an offer to a candidate, you want your candidate to be mentally and emotionally ready to accept. Herein lies another aspect of the recruiter controlling the process. As long as the recruiter has the offer, the recruiter is in control. Once you extend that offer to your candidate, the candidate is in control. So you need to do everything possible to ensure that the candidate accepts.

Yes, we should always be closing….at the initial interview, at the matching call, at every prep and debrief. But that final trial close before actually extending an offer is essential. It is critical. It's that last final "can anything screw this deal up" call that you have to make. It's hard – I get that. You have a client that is ready to make your candidate an offer…they give you the ok to extend the verbal….and all you want to do is call your candidate and give them the offer. Even when, in your heart, you are 100%

confident the candidate will accept the client's offer. Don't. Take a step back and trial close first. On both ends.

On the client side, when they are ready to extend an offer, find out where they would like the offer to be (with respect to money). Once they give you that number, and give you the go-ahead to extend it to your candidate, let them know you are going to reach out one more time to trial close the candidate before actually extending the offer….not that you anticipate anything going wrong, but just to ensure that when we do officially extend the offer, they accept it. Then, ask the client that, in the off chance there are some last-minute things that get in the way, if there is any "wiggle room" in their offer. Not that you will need it…it's just in case.

Then call your candidate. Do NOT let them know you have an offer. Confirm their interest in the position. Confirm the dollar amount that you have by now repeatedly closed them at (and, by the way, that number should always (ideally) be below the offer your client has made). Then, let them know that you are in a *position* to get them an offer. Ask if there is any reason that, if you are able to secure an offer at or above their number, they would not be able to get on the phone that day, call the hiring manager and verbally accept the opportunity. Then listen. Is there hesitation? If so, probe. Is there excitement? If so, rephrase the same question and keep closing...."so, you want me to go and get an offer for you?" Is there still excitement? If so, rephrase the same question and keep closing...."so if I am able to negotiate an offer at or above 'X' there is no reason you can think of why you would not accept it?" ....you get the idea. Seems basic, seems silly, but it is essential if you are going to control and manage the process (the way your client expects you to).

Remember...we get paid to *deliver* candidates. Not simply to find them. Not simply to recruit them. Not simply to set up send outs for them with our clients. We get paid to *deliver* them. Which means that when one of your clients is ready to make an offer to one of your candidates, they are looking to you to manage and control that process. The second you extend a verbal offer to your candidate, you give up control. So why do that if you are not 100%

sure the candidate will accept the offer? Why risk all your hard work and effort during a search without making absolutely positively sure everything is a "go?" Why roll the dice when there is something you can do to remain in control.

Use a 2-step trial close.

Remember...At the end of the placement cycle when we are ready to extend an offer, close one more time before actually extending the offer (even when you have an offer in hand....ESPECIALLY when you have an offer in hand!). Make the call to the candidate and make absolutely sure that (a) they want the opportunity, (2) they want you to get them an offer, (3) you know exactly where they will say yes and where they will say no, and (4) they are ready to immediately call the hiring manager and accept the offer when it is made (and yes, I STILL advocate for this as a step in the process). Then, hang up the phone, and assuming all is in line, call them back in a few minutes, congratulate them, and put them on the phone with the hiring manager to accept. On the flip side, should something come up in that first call, you still have the offer in hand

and are therefore still in control, so you can deal with whatever is on the table *before* you actually extend an offer.

Clients pay us to deliver candidates. When we get to the offer stage, they are counting on us to deliver the candidate they are making an offer to. Control what you can control. Be sure about your candidate. Trial close your candidates before extending offers. Taking the time to do so will improve your chances for success and keep you in control of the situation.

Never, never, never, never (did I say never?) extend an offer to a candidate without trial closing them.

$$$

Money Maker #25: Change the Way You Speak. It Can Make a

BIG Difference!

Recruiting is a business that combines art and science. How we phrase communications with candidates and clients is a significant aspect of the "art" portion of recruiting. We can sound like all the other recruiters on the street, or we can choose to be different. In order to do this, we need to "wordsmith" our delivery to the outside world. I'd like to suggest a couple very small adjustments that can make an exponential difference in the way you are perceived:

#1: Remove "Fit" and "Match" from your vocabulary

"Fit" and "match" are words that recruiters use internally in the office every day. Repeatedly. Over and Over. "My candidate is a perfect match for your job." "Let me see who I have that would be a good fit for that position." While these terms are perfectly fine for use internally when talking with other recruiters and account executives, they tend to be impersonal and robotic-like to the outside world. Clients pay us to deliver talent that will add value to their organization. They do not pay us to simply find a "match" or the right "fit" for their organization. We introduce candidates to opportunities that are in line with their career goals, offer growth, and improve their future marketability. We do not simply tell them about positions for which they would be a good "fit". These are subtle changes in the way we speak. However, if you remove the words "fit" and "match" from your vocabulary when speaking to clients and candidates, I guarantee you that your conversation will be perceived to be a more professional and personalized one. And it will distinguish you from most of your competition. Doing this is not as easy as it sounds. Like anything else, you have to commit to it and make a conscious effort to do it. It is a subtle change that can make an exponential difference.

If you want to find something that "fits," go to a department store. If you want to find a good "match," there are plenty of services in the world that do that.....and none are executive recruiters. But I digress....

#2: Stop saying "I Think"

$$$

Plain and simple, if you remove the words "I think" from the beginning of any sentence, the statement you are making becomes much more confident and powerful. "I think business is good" vs. "Business is good." "I think the market is strong" vs. "The market is strong." "I think this candidate would work well in the role you've described to me" vs. "This candidate would work well in the role you've described to me." "I think this is a great opportunity" vs. "This is a great opportunity." You get the point. It is a subtle change that can make an exponential difference. There's an old saying…if you "think," you don't "know."

Challenge yourself to change the way you speak and make your messages more confident and personal in their delivery. It will make a big difference as to how you are perceived in the market, and will be a huge differentiator from your competitors!

Money Maker #26: Don't Throw Your Leftovers Away!

As I sat eating my lunch one day last week, I started reflecting on the fact that I eat a LOT of leftovers. I love them. I'll eat them for days! My children sometimes cannot believe the leftovers I will consume – items that have been sitting in the refrigerator for probably too long. But hey, I have been known to have an iron stomach...but I digress.

On this particular day in question, the meal I was enjoying was a great combination of chicken, string beans and mashed potatoes. Around my house, I am known as the human garbage disposal....I can't stand to throw food out. So, if it's in the fridge, there's a good chance that I will eat it at some point, even if no one else does.....as long as nothing is growing on it! Hey - I have to draw the line SOME where! But most meals can be re-purposed. Take chicken for example. If I serve a rotisserie chicken one night, any leftover chicken can be become, say, chicken pot pie.....and the carcass can be used to make homemade chicken stock....and I could take some of the leftover meat, combine it with other things and make a killer Panini or quesadilla…..my point being that while my initial purpose for the chicken may have been to carve it and serve with some veggies and a starch for dinner, that alone is not the only use for that chicken. I need to keep on finding uses for the chicken until I no longer have any left.

Where is all this going and how does this tie into the business of recruiting? Read on…

I then began thinking about all the candidates we interview over the course of our recruiting lives. Some good, some bad, some mediocre, some outstanding. Some we place and some we do not. But sometimes, we are too one-dimensional with our thinking when it comes to our candidates. When a company shows interest in one of our candidates we sometimes fall into the mindset that it's the *only* place for that candidate…the *only* use for them. When in reality, if one company likes them, so will others. Also, if a client interviews 4 candidates and hires one, what are we doing with the other 3? Are we proactively finding targets to re-market them? What are we doing with our leftovers? There's always more than one place where a candidate can be marketed and more than one company that would be interested in them. Are we doing all we can to take these candidates to market? Are we reusing and repurposing our leftovers? Or are they rotting in the refrigerator....left to be forgotten or, worse yet, to be gobbled up by our competitors?

We recruit candidates....we submit them to clients.....maybe they interview, maybe they do not.....and often we toss them to the curb. We give up and move on way too quickly and often start over from scratch trying to find more candidates when we still have strong candidates to work with. We go looking for new "food" when there is already "food" in our "fridge" that is perfectly good and can become a "meal" if we just put some thought and effort into it. Remember the phrase, "there is a seat for every butt and a butt for every seat." Words to live by in our business. There is a place for every good candidate we recruit.....keep submitting them.....don't just put all your eggs into one basket....all your hopes on one client or job order. If you have a demand-area candidate, that candidate profile should be marketed everywhere you can think of in your market. Keep marketing your candidates, especially the ones who interview with clients but for one reason or another do not get hired. Market them externally as well as internally to other recruiters on your team. At some point, your candidate leftovers might just turn into a great meal!

Don't throw away your leftovers. If you don't find a use for them, your competition will!

Money Maker #27: Maintain Control and Close the Deal You Can

Close!

You are in a situation where there are multiple offers coming

from several of your clients for one of your candidates......what to

do? What offer do you go after? Where do you close the

candidate...and how? Time for a multiple choice quiz!

Your candidate has three of your clients interested in making them

an offer. You should:

   A. Get offers from all three

   B. Pit all the clients against each other in an all-out bidding war

   C. Step aside and let all the clients negotiate directly with your

      candidate

   D. None of the above

If you chose 'D' you would be correct. Clients pay us to

deliver candidates. Never forget that. If and when we get to offer

stage, and we are suggesting a client extend an offer to our candidate, we are in effect telling that client that if they do extend an offer, we can deliver the candidate to them. So what do you do when you have multiple clients drooling over your one candidate? You stay in control!

In theory, if we are doing our job correctly, we always have a pulse on the candidate. We know what they are looking for, why they are looking for it, what they currently earn, what they are looking to earn.....you get where I am going. I don't think I need to list out the 3,276,481 items of information we need to know in order to control a candidate. If we are doing our job correctly, we have shown the candidate several opportunities that fall in line with what they are looking for. So, what then do we do if the candidate says they like all three, and all three clients want to make an offer to the candidate? We stay in control. We close and deliver the candidate where they are deliverable. Sounds simple enough but so often we fail to do this.

At *every* debrief (that conversation you have with your candidate after every client interview), have the candidate rank the opportunities in order of preference. Then, when it comes to getting an offer, simply go after the offer at the opportunity they want most. If they are non-committal, ask them, "Money aside – if all three companies extended offers at the exact same dollar amount – where do you want to be?" Take money out of the equation and continue to focus on what the candidate wants in an opportunity. If they are still non-committal or tell you that they want to see what the offers are, remind them that you are not in the business of getting offers for the candidate to think about or consider. You are in the business of getting offers your candidate will accept. Let them know in no uncertain terms that the client is looking to you for guidance, and they will not extend an offer unless you give them the go-ahead and assurance that the candidate will accept. This can be a difficult conversation to have with a candidate, but if you have laid the groundwork and explained how the process works (from the start, from the initial interview you had with that candidate), it should not be an issue. And it keeps you in control of the situation.

$$$

Find out where the candidate wants to be. Get them to commit to accepting an offer from THAT opportunity and take the focus off all others. Then, go and get THAT offer and deliver them to THAT opportunity. Period. Don't make this business harder than it has to be. If you start getting multiple offers then inevitably money becomes the driving factor, not opportunity; and it can cloud your candidate's vision. Stay focused and stay in control. As long as YOU hold the cards, YOU are in control. The second you extend an offer to your candidate, control shifts from you to them, so you want to be sure they are going to say yes to the offer you extend.

If we are working smart and marketing your best candidates to hiring managers in your market, this situation should happen often. That would be a good thing. Just remember, stay in control. Close your candidate first and then get the offer at the opportunity they want most. And close the deal!

Money Maker #28: Always Be Prepared....Go 5 Deep!

Clients pay us to deliver candidates. You probably are used

to this as a recurring theme I have. But it's true and cannot be

emphasized enough. Clients count on us to have access to

candidates in the market that they do not have access

to. *Candidates. Plural,* not singular. You and I know that if and

when we execute our jobs perfectly, we take a job order, introduce

the client to one candidate that is right for the role, and they hire that

candidate. We like that scenario! Unfortunately, most placement

cycles do not happen that way. We try to hit a bull's-eye on the first

pass but that one candidate is not always the winner. If we are

prepared and if we are proactive in our job, this should never slow us

down. So often I hear, "We've presented one candidate...client

loves them....but they want to see more resumes before they will

begin interviewing." Now, granted, some of this is client control,

but I won't go there right now. That is another Money Maker all

together! When this happens, most of the time we are faced with the

challenge of working against the clock (and our competition) to recruit additional candidates for a job order. We have one, but we don't have multiple. And time passes.....and more time passes......and time kills all deals. My advice? Always go 5 deep with your candidates and this will not happen.

5 Deep. It's a great concept. Within your demand area (for accounting & finance this would be the candidate profiles of Staff Accountant, Senior Accountant and Financial Analyst) and even slightly outside of it (for accounting & finance this would be Accounting Manager, Controller) we should all strive to maintain an inventory "hot list" whereby we constantly have 5 fee-worthy candidates at the ready in each category. Because of the nature of our industry, candidates will activate, get placed, find jobs on their own, come off the market, etc., so this list is not static. It is ever changing and, as a result, we need to always be proactively recruiting talent to keep the inventory at max capacity. Whether you have open job orders or not for certain profiles is not the point. *Proactively* recruit talent. Don't *reactively* recruit talent for job orders. The latter is too short-sighted and will not lead you to

the Promised Land. If you always have strong talent in your network, you will always be prepared for job orders when you get them. And if you are disciplined enough to focus a majority of your recruiting and marketing efforts (say, 70% or more) in similar profile areas, you will always be in the game. You will always have a shot at a fee. If not? Well.....

Go 5 deep and you will always be prepared for job orders that come in the door!

Money Maker #29: The More You Know…..The More You Know!

While some may say ignorance is bliss, in our world ignorance is unacceptable.

In our world, while we are not expected to be technical experts in the verticals we recruit for (I, for example, will never be an accountant). We *are* expected to be experts in the industry of recruiting. Clients and candidates expect us to know what we are talking about….to know the ins and outs and all the little details that they would not – and could not – uncover on their own. They expect us to know more because we are the experts. Think about it…..if I am feeling under the weather, and I do some online research and find several possible diagnoses that seem to fit my symptoms, that's still not as good (or as reassuring) as going to a doctor, having them examine me, run tests and return a diagnosis. Why? Because when I go to the doctor, I expect that they will know more than I do about medical concerns. I expect more from them…and thus I pay them for their service to know I have received the best care. I pay for the peace of mind of going to an expert and getting results.

$$$

The world of recruiting is similar. Clients can hire employees on their own. Candidates can search for opportunities on their own. The means exist to do both. However, they are not experts in doing so. We are….or at least that's what we proclaim. In order to earn that tag, we have to demonstrate our expertise – one candidate, one client, one placement cycle at a time. And with each cycle….each candidate in play….each job order…each client…we need to challenge ourselves to always know more than everyone else involved. We should always know more about the candidate than the client who is interviewing them. We should always know more about the client than the candidate who is interviewing with them. We should know more because it's our job to know more. Period.

To do this, remember to always **QUERY**:

Question: Question everything. Ask, listen, and ask some more. The only way to learn is to ask questions.

Understand: It's not always enough to get responses to questions. You have to understand the response. Sometimes this involves additional research on your part (see "ask more questions").

Educate: Always strive to increase your knowledge, and not just academically. Read papers, industry periodicals, blogs...watch cable news channels...know a little about as much as you can! And know even more about companies you are doing business with, their industry, current and forecasted trends and potential effects on them.

Research: Technology has made it very easy to do research. There is no excuse for not being extensively well versed in your client companies before even talking to a candidate about considering to interview with them. There is also no reason why you should not know your candidates before you even meet them. Google them. Google your clients. Google your hiring managers. Look all of them up on LinkedIn. Look them up on Hoovers. Read the press releases on their corporate websites. You see where I am going.....

$$$

You: It is up to you. *You* must take responsibility to always know

more than the parties you are

dealing with. Take it upon yourself to become the more

knowledgeable party and you will clearly distinguish yourself as the

expert....and earn respect from all.

Whenever we need answers we tend to go to the person we

believe has the most knowledge in that particular area. We go to the

person who should have the answers. Be *that* person. Know

more. Because the more you know....the more you know!

$$$

Money Maker #30: Be a Connector!

I once met with the Principle of a small but growing web development company in Annapolis, MD. I met with her because she was referred to me directly by several people who I knew from a technology networking organization I was heavily involved with. I was connected to her from a contact I initially made 5 years prior. That connection lead me to a new client and a new job order. It reinforced to me why we need to always be connecting to other people. You never know who or where or when you will get something out of it. In this case, my connection was made as a result of another connection I had made long ago....and still stay connected with. Because that's what we should do.

There's an old saying, "It's not what you know, it's who you know" that holds true to some extent in every profession – arguably none more than recruiting. We make our living based on who we know. We end up knowing some people very well based on deepened relationships we form while working with them, and we need to know as many of them as possible in order to be successful. We need a vast network of people we can continually connect with in order to get what we need for our clients. We need to be connected. More specifically, we need to be connectors.

Connectors, as defined by Malcolm Gladwell in his book "The Tipping Point," are people with a special gift of bringing the world together. They know a lot of people and, over time as their network continues to grow, they become the go-to people when information is needed. In your market, you should want to become this person. You want people in your market and in your space to not only be in your book of business but to look to you for guidance, advice and information about their career, the market, and even specific companies. You want your clients to look to you first before others in our industry because you are the recruiter they feel has the deepest contacts. You are the one they can trust to find that needle in the haystack, because you have proven to them you "know everyone" in the market and that your network is the deepest. You are the most connected.

$$$

Connecting. Think about it. It is at the core of everything we do. We connect with candidates, we connect with clients, we connect them to each other, and we look to them to connect us to more contacts through referrals. We need to be connectors in order to be the best in our business.

The world is composed of a bunch of dots....connect them!

Money Maker #31:   Reading is Fundamental....and Necessary!

Read. Your teachers used to tell you to do it. Maybe your parents told you to do it. But did you?

When I was a kid, reading for me meant the sports page in the Washington Post. But, as Katy Perry says, "That was then and this is now." Once I joined the professional workforce, I learned very quickly that in order to increase my vocabulary and keep up with business goings on, I needed to read. It was then that I realized there were more sections to the newspaper....there was actually a 'business' section....and a front-page 'A' section. Imagine my surprise when I learned there was more to life than the Washington Redskins and the Maryland Terrapins! ....but I digress.

When you are in school, you read because you are told to. You are required to. Well, in the professional workforce, while no one is going to give you a test (wait, there's a thought!), you should read because you *want* to and also because, in order to be at the top of your game.... you *need* to.

$$$

In our business, we interact and converse with a myriad of people from all walks of life. We have clients across a plethora of industries. And we are perceived to be experts in all things associated with employment and staffing. That's a tall order to live up to. So what's one way we can create and live up to that perception? Read.

Challenge yourself to know a little about a lot of topics so that you are able to engage in conversations at networking functions, over the phone, during client visits, in candidate interviews….you get the idea. What to read? There are many answers to that, and I would argue that it should be a constant combination of personal and professional reading. Some guidelines to consider (and this is by no means a complete list):

- Read books. You should always be reading a book. And it does not have to always be a professional / business oriented book. Personally, I alternate my reading. When I complete a business book, I move on to a novel or some other non-business type of book. Once I complete that, I will start another business book, and so on. Reading books stimulates your mind and has been proven to have a direct correlation to intelligence and an increased vocabulary. Now, time tends to be a factor....it does takes time to read. Make time to read. And don't feel like you have to read the whole book – or even a whole chapter – in one sitting. Hold yourself accountable to read at least 2-3 pages per day. If you have time for more, great. But if not, you can always find time for a few pages.

- Read your local paper. Yes the paper – either online or in print. You should be up to date on local happenings in your community/town/city so that you can talk about them with the people you interact with.

- Diversify your reading. Know a little about current sporting events, government happenings, international goings on, local news.....try to be aware about a lot. You do not have to have in-depth knowledge, but you should have a high-level general understanding of things so that you can discuss when

you find yourself in a position to do so.

- Read your local business journal. Go to

www.bizjournals.com. If your market has a business journal,

make sure you subscribe. It is a weekly publication that

covers business issues in your local market. You can learn a

lot and get great leads from the business journals. At that

website you can also subscribe to a free daily/weekly online

newsletter that will go directly into your inbox.

- Read the Wall Street Journal. Yes, even if you do not work

in New York City, the WSJ is a good paper to read,

especially for all news financial.

- Read industry trades. Be sure to bookmark

www.staffingtoday.net, www.staffingindustry.com, and

www.americanstaffing.net so that you can stay abreast of

what is going on within the staffing and recruiting industry.

- Read the reports form the Bureau of Labor Statistics

(www.bls.gov). The current local and national

unemployment rates, jobs report, and other reports that impact our industry can be found there.

- Read client industry trades. If you have a high concentration of a particular industry within your market, find out what trade magazines your clients read….and read them.

- Read what your mentors read. Talk to people in business that you respect, both within and outside the recruiting industry, and ask them what they read.

There are more, but that is a start. The good news is that you can sign up for so many industry feeds online, thereby making it easy for you to keep up with all the pertinent news automatically and on a consistent basis. They key is to actually read those feeds when they come to you.

Read. It is a fundamental key to anyone's success. Make it part of yours!

Money Maker #32: A Handful of Key Questions to Ask Your Candidate!

Not every deal closes. Some fall apart. And after a deal does go south, so to speak, it is always a good idea to analyze it and explore if and how you could have done something different that might have affected the outcome. When you do this, you will inevitably realize moments where you neglected to ask some tough questions that might have made a difference. Might have. Granted, in our world, there are times when we do everything "right" and the deal still does not go through. Sometimes life happens and we cannot stop it. But in most situations, we can take certain measures to influence the course of action and maintain control. Here are some questions that you should be asking your candidates (if you are not already doing so):

Question #1: "What else do you have going on right now, and where are you in the process?"

We should always know where else our candidate has sent their resume, where else they are interviewing, and if it is on their own accord or through another recruiter. We also need to know what stage they are at in other cycles. First interview? Offer pending? It makes a difference, and we need to be aware. Plus, this can provide us with good job leads as well, so there are multiple reasons for asking this particular question.

Question #2: "How does this opportunity (your client) compare to the others you are considering?"

Notice I did not ask, "Do you have any other opportunities in play?" Never assume yours is the only opportunity a candidate is considering. Hopefully, we have had an open and direct line of communication; and if there are other opportunities on the table, we are aware of them. In addition to simply knowing about those other opportunities, we need to know where our opportunity "ranks" in comparison.

Question #3: "Money aside, where do you want to be? Meaning, if both companies made you offers at the same dollar amount, which would be your #1 choice?"

$$$

This is used when a candidate is not willing to show their hand between multiple opportunities they are exploring, either all with you or some with you. This is a similar question to #2 above, and can be a good follow-up to that question if they are vague with their initial answer. We are trying to determine where they prefer to work, and if an offer was made, would they accept it. We are looking for a commitment either way. Even a commitment toward another opportunity (not yours) is better than no commitment at all. At least you will know where you stand.

Question #4: (In the event your opportunity is *not* the candidate's #1 choice) Is there anything my client could do that would turn their opportunity from #2 to #1 in your mind?"

Sometimes our opportunity is simply not going to be as strong as something else a candidate is looking at. Even if it is not their initial first choice, we need to explore ways in which it could potentially become their first choice. Do not accept defeat without a fight. Sometimes, by asking this simple question we can turn a #2 opportunity into #1. Also, it is important to ask this question and get all your ducks in a row BEFORE you go to your client and ask for

something....or something more. You only want to go to the well

once; and when you do, you had better be sure that if your client

gives you what you ask for, you can deliver your candidate.

Question #5: (If your opportunity *is* their #1 choice) "If I am

able to get you an offer at 'x' or better, are you prepared to pick

up the phone, call the hiring manager, accept the offer today,

and turn off all other opportunities you are currently involved

with?"

The answer we are looking for to this question is

"yes." Nothing else. Not "I'm pretty sure I would" or "I think so"

…. Just "yes." Anything else means your candidate is not

closed. We do not want to ask our client for an offer unless we are

sure our candidate will say yes to it. Immediately. If they need time

to think about it, we have to first ask why and then give them time to

think *before* we actually get and give them an offer. Have them

come back to you and tell you whether or not they want you to get

them an offer, knowing that if you do, you will expect them to say yes and verbally accept immediately. As long as WE have the offer in hand, WE are in control. The second we give that offer to our candidate, we LOSE control. At that point, THEY are in control. So, we want to be as sure as humanly possible that they are ready to say yes.

Question #6: "This opportunity is contingent on a credit, criminal and drug screen. Is there anything I should be aware of?"

This is a nice way of asking your candidate if they have any past crimes, credit flags or drug usage that would show up on a test or background check. By asking this question, you are giving them an opportunity to come clean. If they do have something to be aware of, it gives you a chance to give your client a heads up. Things can show up on credit and criminal checks that may have happened many years ago...but they still could show up. Depending on the severity, we can sometimes alert our client to what may show up and why it may show up; and when it does, since we were up front about it, it may not affect the offer. When we do not disclose information, and the client is surprised by it, there is a perception that we or the candidate (or both) were trying to hide something. That can definitely put an offer in jeopardy. We don't want that.

There are obviously many more questions we can and should be asking candidates – throughout the entire placement process. The above are some that stand out to me. We work too hard to put ourselves in a position to win. Let's make sure we continue to ask the tough questions, especially as we get near the finish line.

$$$

Money Maker #33: Preserve Your Investment: The Post Placement Follow-up!

Congratulations - you just made a placement! What will you do next? Shout out, "I'm going to Disney World?" Well, while you might do that, it's not exactly the next step in the process. The deal is not done. As a matter of fact, far from it.

We invest a lot of time and energy during a placement process. When we are successful and the deal goes through, it is not the end of the process but, rather, a new beginning. It marks a time when we can strengthen our relationship with our client and our candidate, as well as a time when we should take all steps necessary to preserve and protect our investment. Not only should you want to make sure all goes well during your guarantee period and that you collect your fee from the client, you should make sure that all parties do not forget about you. The moment a candidate accepts an opportunity with one of your clients is a time when all parties involved are happy...there is collective enthusiasm...and it is a prime opportunity for you to get more business (either in the form of leads, referrals and more job orders).

While there are important steps we have to manage from the time we submit a candidate to the time they accept an offer, what we do *after* that is equally as important. The following communication and steps (at a minimum) are suggested:

- Coach your candidate through the resignation and notice period. Remember that counter offers usually do not happen on the day a candidate gives notice. It can, and typically, happen at some point during their notice period....right up until the last hour of their last work day. Candidates need to know that. Make sure there is absolutely nothing their current employer can do to keep them.

- Call your candidate the day/night before they are scheduled to resign.

- Have your candidate call you as soon as they give notice.

- Take your candidate to lunch midway through their notice period. Call it a celebratory lunch and use the opportunity to make sure they are still on board, a source for referrals, and understand what they should expect in their new opportunity.

- Call your candidate the evening before the first day of their new job.
- Call your candidate at the end of the day of Day 1.
- Call your candidate on the Friday at the end of Week 1.

Call your candidate at Month 1, Month 2, Month 3, Month 6, and Month 12. Do this for several reasons. Yes, you want to make sure they last through your guarantee period and that there are no yellow or red flags during their initial time with your client, but you also so that they *remember* you. If we do not stay in touch, they will forget. How many times have you interviewed a candidate who was placed by a recruiter...and they cannot remember the recruiter's name? Don't be that recruiter. If you maintain communication during the post-placement period, they will always remember you. And they'll appreciate it. And they'll continue to forget about your competition!

$$$

With the technology available to us (Outlook, Gmail, contact management systems, etc.) it is very easy to set these reminders as soon as you know the candidate's start date. Make it easy for yourself and set them as soon as the deal is done.

Sidebar....if you make a placement, suggest a client lunch on the Friday following the candidate's first week of employment to discuss how they are performing and acclimating to the job. Oh, and while you are there, let them know you'd be happy to pick up your check so that your client preserves their investment during the guarantee period. Seriously, you'd be surprised how often that works....and money in the door = you getting paid. Just sayin'...

Manage the post placement portion of your deals. It can be a huge difference maker!

Money Maker #34: The Takeaway!

If you love something, set it free. If it comes back to you, it was meant to be and if not….well, not so much. We've heard that saying before – most of the time with respect to personal relationships. And we can certainly apply it to recruiting because after all, ours *is* a business of relationships, right?

In life, we are so afraid to ask the tough questions because we are afraid we will not hear the answer we want to hear. But the answer we *need* to hear is the truth. And sometimes, to get to the truth, you have to ask tough questions. When closing deals – on both the candidate and the client side – this very often comes into play. One of those tough questions, or strategies, that is extremely effective when closing is a technique known as "the takeaway." The takeaway is a great litmus test to determine if the party you are working with is truly committed to what is going on. It can help you sense the levels of urgency on both sides of the equation. And it helps you determine where your focus should be and where to spend your time.

Some examples of using the takeaway:

1) Candidate example: You have the lead candidate in an interview cycle with your client and your client wants to make them an offer. Your candidate has 2 other interviews (not through you) lined up, and they are saying they want to see them through before entertaining any offers.

The takeaway: "Understand that we are in a position right now to go after an offer with Company A. However, as discussed, I am not going to go after that offer unless you want it and are ready to accept it. If you are, great. If not, and you want to see those other interviews through and hope for something better, just understand that this opportunity will most likely be gone. What would you like to do?"

If the candidate lets you take it away, they really don't want the opportunity. If they want it, they will cancel the other interviews and go after the offer.

2) Client Example: Your candidate just finished interviewing with your client, and you are debriefing with the client. The client tells you that while they like your candidate and want you to keep them warm, but they need to see more candidates (how many times have we heard *THAT*?). The takeaway: "Understand that this candidate is actively interviewing with some of your competitors in the market. If we do not move on them this week, there is a good chance they will not be available to consider. What would you like to do?"

If your client lets you take the candidate away, they really didn't want to hire them. If they are interested, they will move the process forward.

When you use the takeaway technique, and the person you are working with lets you take it away, having backup prevents you from going into a panic. You see, if you have the #1 and #2 candidates in a placement cycle (that's another Money Maker!), and they let you take away #1, you move on #2. No ground lost. When you only have one candidate in play, you get burned. Same on the candidate side of the house. If you have a fee-worthy candidate, and you only present one opportunity to them instead of getting them involved with multiple clients, you cling to that one. Take it away and you have nothing. But having several opportunities in play, you can always redirect to opportunity #2.

Be a better closer. Ask tough questions. Use the takeaway.

$$$

Money Maker #35: The Million Dollar Marketing Question!

Marketing calls. We make a lot of them every day. Some

end up leading to job orders, some do not. And in some cases we

hang up the phone feeling like we just couldn't convince our

audience that they should use our services. We've said things like

"We are contingent....it doesn't cost you a cent unless you hire from

us.... just take a look."......you name it, we've said it. And we still

couldn't get the prospect over that hump. We could not get them to

see the *value* we offer. Did we do anything wrong? Not

necessarily. But did we do everything possible to enlighten

them? Maybe...or maybe not. In every conversation you always

need that one key phrase that is almost a lock to get things going in

the right direction. Kind of like when I was a night club DJ in

college....there was always that one song that was guaranteed to get

people dancing, and on slow nights, I would whip it out and it would

always work.....but I digress.

In marketing situations, when calling a hiring manager and trying to

earn their business, there exists such a phrase that is very effective.

"How important is it for you to hire the best talent the market has to offer?"

That, my friends, is the million-dollar marketing question. Why? Because more often than not, it will solicit a positive response from a hiring manager, extend your conversation, and allow you to educate your audience as to why working with you will allow them to do just that. You will be able to plant that little seed of doubt that they may not find what they want on their own, as well as discussing the *value* you can add to their business by introducing them to talent that is beyond their reach. Most companies subscribe to job boards. What they do not often realize, and what you need to educate them on, is that while they will get strong response to their ads, the overwhelming majority of the candidates that respond to those ads are active candidates – professionals that are actively seeking employment – and unemployed candidates. In most professional lines of business, the true number of the unemployed that are looking actively is about 2-4%. By working with a professional recruiter, who targets passive candidates (i.e., those not aggressively looking but would consider making a career move for the right opportunity), a company can gain access to the other 96-98% of the talent market.

Take this scenario for example: Let's say a company ran an ad for a Staff Accountant. You, being the exceptional recruiter that you are, make an MPC call into that hiring manager and market a stunning Staff Accountant profile. The hiring manager tells you that while the profile sounds impressive, they just ran the ad and therefore need to see what it returns first before considering going to a recruiter. Here's your moment....

You then ask the hiring manager, "How important is it for you to hire the best talent the market has to offer?" The hiring manager replies, "Very important." Ah....now it's time to educate the hiring manager. "I understand you want the best the market has to offer. Are you aware that the response you get from your ad typically comes from the unemployed talent base? Nationally, the unemployment rate for degreed accounting professionals is less than 4%. Therefore, your ad will yield the best talent of that 4%, which is not necessarily the best talent on the market. Our candidates are

passive, meaning, they are not aggressively seeking employment but,

for the right opportunity, would consider making a move. They are

not responding to ads. They are performing job functions at other

companies – often at your competitors – and work through us to

explore specific opportunities. Your ad is not reaching that talent

base. Let me make a suggestion….compare our best against your

ad's best. If you find better talent from your ad, hire them – I

would. At least you will have peace of mind knowing that you have

explored the market thoroughly. If you decide to hire someone

through us, then you will owe us a fee for services. However, keep

in mind that our services are contingent. You do not pay unless you

actually hire someone from us. It costs you nothing but an

investment of time to meet with our candidates. The pressure is on

us to deliver talent that is far superior to anything you are seeing

from your ad. We assume all the risk."

$$$

Before you give up and walk away from an opportunity, make sure you use all the tools in your toolbox. One of those tools should be the million dollar marketing question!

Oh…and for the record, my 'go to' song was "Let The Music Play" by Shannon.

$$$

Money Maker #36: The Million Dollar Recruiting Question!

Wouldn't it be great if, just like there exists a million dollar marketing question, there was an equally as effective question you could use during a recruiting call that could extend the conversation and improve your chances for landing the recruit? Wouldn't it be great if every passive candidate we called recognized the value we, as recruiters, bring to the table – regardless of whether we have a position of interest for them right now or not?

We make a lot of recruiting calls every day – or at least we should. We should constantly be recruiting for (a) hot open job orders that need coverage and (b) inventory within our demand area. The latter is sometimes a more challenging recruiting call because you are calling an attractive, passive candidate with no active job order on the docket who on the surface, seems like it would be of interest. This, my friends, is exactly where you test your recruiting skills. If you can get someone to meet with you without having an opportunity for them right now, then, in my opinion, you are truly a good recruiter. So what do you say on those calls? There are many approaches that work, and no one method or word track is necessarily right or wrong. When I am sensing hesitation from my audience, I tend to throw a question out there that solicits a "yes" response and then explain what I do for a living in an effort to gain their buy in to the process....and to me. At some point in the recruiting call, when you encounter resistance, try this....

"If there was an opportunity in the market that was far superior to your current position, and could improve your life personally, professionally and financially, would you want to hear about it? Notice I did not say a "better" opportunity....I said "far superior." I also further dramatized it by referencing a person's personal, professional and financial well-being. This is no accident.

That, my friends, is the million-dollar recruiting question. Why? Because in most instances, the person on the other end of the phone will answer "yes" to that question. At that point, I explain what I do....that I work with employed professionals like them who do not have to make a move but would at least like the opportunity to hear about what's out there in the event that their dream job surfaces....that I invest my time with people I feel have marketable skills and future potential...and that I learn what they do, where they are and where they want to take their career...and I try to get them there a little faster. It is a very non-threatening approach. And notice at no time did I pitch them "the perfect job." This is because, at this initial stage, I don't know them...and therefore could not possibly suggest that an opportunity would be perfect for them. I have to earn that right. And before I earn that right, I have to meet with them and get to know them. And in order to do that, I have to give them a reason to want to meet with me.

And that's where the million-dollar recruiting question can help. Use it. See what happens.

$$$

Money Maker #37: When Going After Ads, Persistence Wins!

Persistence. It is a trait much needed in our business yet one that is not widespread. That, however, is good news for you! Most of your competition does not have the "sticktoitiveness" (ok, not a real word but one that sounds good and gets the point across) when it comes to marketing, which means it is much easier to beat them to business than you may think.

Maybe Thomas Edison said it best when he said, "Our greatest weakness lies in giving up. The most certain way to succeed is always to try just one more time." Mind you, Edison tried and failed a gazillion (again, not a real word but it sounds good and gets the point across) times. But in all his tries and persistence, he invented things that have become staples in our lives and were critical to our evolution as a society. Now, I am not saying that your persistence as a recruiter will have a huge impact on our society, but then again, if it means landing a job order and filling it with talent that advances someone's career and helps a business succeed, one never knows what impact persistence as a recruiter can have!

As soon as a company posts an ad for a job opening, every recruiter on earth (ok, maybe not on earth, but you get the idea) will be calling that company in an effort to land that job order. Fast forward one week, and statistics show that half of those recruiters give up. Fast forward still another week, and half the remaining recruiters give up. This trend continues week after week. Therefore, the more persistence you have to continue marketing to those hiring managers, the more the possibility exists that (a) they will start to remember you and (b) they will give you a shot at filling the job. Or, at a minimum, they will be impressed with your persistence and just might be willing to open a dialogue and consider doing business with you in the future. The key to making all this happen is persistence. In your call plans, call about these ads week after week with consistency until you know the position has been filled. Don't give up after one phone call. Be part of the recruiting group that moves forward each week, not the one that drops off.

"Chasing Ads" is an activity that is part of every executive recruiter's daily plan (or at least it should be). These are what are commonly referred to as 'hunting' calls since there is a known opening in the market and, if successful at earning the business, offers an opportunity to make a placement right away...now ... to 'put food on the table' (hence the 'hunting' analogy). These are calls that involve consistent, planned follow-up and persistence. Those who do this will have a higher chance of improving their personal brand in the market. Those who call on an ad once and then toss it to the curb get nothing. Nada. Nil.

As with any call, there are a number of things that can be accomplished/gained/learned from ad calls - more so than simply landing a job order. It is a good reminder to us that we need to multi-purpose every call we make. Each call we make is a *recruiting* call and a *marketing* call. Every call. Without exception. Too often we go into calls with one objective and one of two things usually happens: Either we (a) accomplish that objective and end the call; or (b) we do not accomplish that objective and end the call. I would argue that in both cases, the recruiter has failed. As a wise person once told me, "If you go into a call looking to accomplish 'x' and you accomplish 'x,' you have failed."

Back to ad calls for a moment....

If the position is still open when you make the call, some things you should be asking include:

- Why is the position open?

- How long has it been open?

- If the ad does not yield the talent they want, what actions are they prepared to take?

- What is the cost of not filling the open position? Who is doing the work now?

- When would they ideally like to have the position filled?

- Have they/do they utilize recruiting firms

Yes, there are more questions to ask, but that is a good start.

If the position has been filled, some things we should be asking include:

- Why was the position open?

- How long was it open?

- How did they find the candidate they hired?

- Has the person started (or when are they scheduled to start)?

- If the new hire is already on board, how are things going?

- Have they/do they utilize recruiting firms?

Again, there are more questions to ask, but that is a good start.

Now, if the position has been filled and filled very recently, we have an opportunity to dig for some serious leads:

- Where did the person come from (the company, not the recruiting firm)? There is now a vacancy at that company.

  LEAD!

- Where did the person go (we know this of course because we are calling the company they were hired by)? There is now a new contact at a company, possibly at a hiring manager level.

  LEAD!

- When did the person start? The first 3 months on the job are volatile and they may not work out.

  LEAD!

- How did the person get there? Did the company pay a fee for them? If so, you have just confirmed that company as a qualified prospect for future marketing .

LEAD!

When you come across a candidate who is new in a position, or when you talk with a hiring manager who has just made a hire, you should always try to find out this information. Within this conversation are leads. Capture the information and act upon the leads.

Make ad calls every week, and push yourself to get as much information out of those calls as possible. Just as you should for every call you make. Edison had a lot of persistence and I'd say it paid off for him. It can pay off for you as well!

$$$

Money Maker #38: Use...I Mean REALLY Use...Your LinkedIn
Connections!

By now you have probably realized that I am a sports fan,

and one of my favorite sports is NFL football. The NFL draft has

many rounds....or levels...to it. Players who are drafted in the first

round are players that are expected to have superior talent. They are

the ones everyone is looking at under a microscope and that every

team is targeting. But every year, there are players selected in the

2nd round (and well beyond!) that turn out to be outstanding

professional athletes. LinkedIn is similar to the NFL draft. While

we are always making those coveted first level connections, there is

much talent beyond that. How often do we ever truly look beyond

the first level? Or, more importantly, do we ever use those

connections for what they are intended to be, which is networking

vehicles to lead us to more talent? Many times while conducting a

search, we go to LinkedIn and run an advanced search. We input

criteria and get a massive subset of people who have what we are, on

the surface, looking for. These people could be first level

connections or they could be far removed. We retrieve them all and we begin cold calling into their companies and trying to talk with them about an opportunity. We might get voice mail and leave a message saying something along the lines of, "I found you on LinkedIn." While this is a decent method of LinkedIn recruiting, we could make our job much easier by making better use of our first level connections. True, we sometimes look into the connections of our first level connections, and we sometimes call those people and reference that we share a common connection. This is good, but the call could be much warmer if we use LinkedIn like it was intended.

Next time you run an advanced search, try this. Limit your search to only first and second level connections. Should you see a second level connection that you want to reach out to, look to see which of your first level connections you are linked through. Then, call that first level connection and inquire as to the relationship they have with the second level connection. If they know the person (perhaps they used to work with them), ask if you can use their name when calling them. This way, when you then call your second level connection to discuss an opportunity you are recruiting for, you can reference the common connection's name, say that you were speaking with them and they referred you to them. Wow...that call just got a LOT warmer! Doing this involves an extra call – NOT an extra email – but hey, isn't being on the phone and networking with people what our job is all about?

Another great aspect of LinkedIn is the section on the right hand margin that shows other profiled that are similar to the one currently being viewed. Chances are, these are also people you want to connect with and get to know. Look for a common thread and try to connect with them.

Finally, go beyond the electronic interface. When you make a first level connection, call them. How often do we accept invitations, or someone accepts ours, and it ends there? Or, we then send them an email and wait for them to respond. We are recruiters, people. Once a connection is made, pick up the phone and call that connection. Engage them in conversation as to how the two of you can help each other and work together. LinkedIn is a networking site. So network! And don't tell me you cannot call them because their phone number is not listed on their profile. The name of their current employer is, right? You have Google, right? Enough said.

LinkedIn is a business networking site. Use it. Don't just *make* first level connections. Use those connections to help your business!

$$$

Money Maker #39: Don't Overthink the Business!

Paralysis by analysis. It is a phenomenon that occurs in many industries and recruiting is no exception. If you are an analytical, you may have a tendency to 'over think' situations. There is an old saying, "Don't think, just do" and there is some truth in that. Now, I'm not saying don't think at all. By all means...think! Just don't *over* think.

It is very easy to over think the business of recruiting. There are so many moving parts, so many unique scenarios that take place simply because our product is human. Still, ours is, in essence, a very simple business. We make placements and put temps to work. Plain and simple. Let's not forget that and remember that everything we do, day in and day out is in motion to the ultimate goals of placements and temp starts. So, always remember:

For the recruiting/candidate side of our business:

If you encounter a person (candidate) who works within your operating space, **talk to them**.

If they sound halfway decent (or better), **meet with them**.

If they are impressive, **market them**.

If they are motivated, **place them**! (before your competitor does)

For the marketing/client side of our business:

If there is a business in your geographic market, **talk to them**.

If there is potential for business, now or in the future, **meet with them**.

When you encounter exceptional talent, **market to them**.

If they are hiring, **make placements** with them! (before your competitor does)

Remarkably similar, yes? That's because both sides of our business – client and candidate – run parallel. We do many of the same things on both sides of the equation, we just tailor those actions to the audience we are directing it to. Sounds simple and straight forward - and it is. We sometimes make it harder than it has to be.

Keep things simple. Don't overthink the business.

Money Maker #40: Ratios - Know How Much You Need To Be Doing!

How well do you know your business? I mean *really* know

your business? No, *really, really* know your business? Ok, point

made. My guess is, probably not as well as you could or

should. And that's ok – most of us fall into that category at some

point in our career. They key is not to stay in that category for very

long.

In our world we constantly have to balance quality with

quantity. But knowing how much *quantity* you need in order to

reach the necessary *quality* levels you need is mission critical to

achieving success....and critical to knowing if you are doing enough

in order to put yourself in a position to be successful. In our

business, it's all about the send out (for perm) and the start (for

staffing). If we do not get to that point in the placement cycle, we

have no chance. We got nuttin. Zero. Squadoosh. Nil. Everything

we do has to be geared toward the ultimate goal of making

placements and putting out temps. To get there, we need send outs and starts. But how much activity does it take to get there each month? That's where you need to know your stuff.

How many of you know your market ratios? Bear with me, because I am going to talk like a perm guy for the moment....only 'cause I am one. To those on the temp side of the house, in the immortal words of Vito Corleone, "I mean no disrespect."

To know what you need to be doing you have to know your market ratios. Here's where the "science" part of recruiting comes into play a bit. How many send outs does it typically take before a placement is made in your market? When I started out, the ratio was 8 to 1 in my market. And, almost like clockwork, for every 8 send outs I was involved with, I'd make a placement. So, I knew if I wanted to make 3 placements in a given month, I needed to be a part of 24 send outs - if I was going to be in a position, statistically, to do so. Key market ratios that are important to know include:

- Candidate interview to submission/presentation ratio
- Candidate submission/presentation to send out ratio
- Send out to placement ratio

$$$

- Average fee amount

Think about it. If I know, on average, how many send outs it takes before making a placement, and how many submissions it takes before I can expect a send out, and how many candidates I typically need to interview before I have one strong enough and fee-worthy to submit to a client, I can then build very effective and efficient call plans designed to generate such activity and results. Knowing this information and using it to drive your desk activity will help you to work more efficiently and put you in a much stronger position to maximize your chances for success....and for making money!

The more you know, the more you know. Be sure you know what you are doing....and why you are doing it!

$$$

Money Maker #41: Little Things Can Mean A Lot!

You've heard it a million times….."It's the little things that mean the most." The sun rising, telling someone you love them, making (and eating!) homemade pie. Yes, little things can mean a lot. So how does this relate to recruiting? Well, in many, many ways. But the way I am thinking of is in fee negotiations.

Think percentage points. Most perm recruiters (and their clients) tend to think in terms of 30-25-20 when it comes to fee percentages. A 30% fee seems like a lost art. Yet retained search firms still routinely charge 33.3%. Some clients seem to think 20% is high. Those are clients who do not see the value in what recruiters offer. All too often we tend to cave due to pressure put on us by market competitors who, by the way, aren't always delivering to the customer….so why do we feel the pressure? You get what you pay for, right? Anyway…. Between 30 and 25 percent, and between 25 and 20 percent, there are a lot of percentage points. And those little points can make a big difference in your fee (and your commission!). For example, a 20% fee on a $60,000 position would be $12,000. Not a bad fee (is *any* fee really *ever* bad?) but just think if you were to negotiate that fee up to 22% instead of 20%. The client sees that as only a 2% increase, yet, while it represents a 2 percentage point increase, it is really a 10% monetary increase. If we simply try to get those 2 percentage points, it takes that $12K fee up to $13,200. Now, $1,200 may not seem like a lot (since when!). However, if your entire recruiting team commits to trying – I mean really trying – to get those extra 2 percentage points on every negotiation, it could add hundreds of thousands of dollars to your gross profit tally. That's not so little.

A bigger fee potential is more worth your recruiting time and effort than a smaller fee (duh!). So why not try to get some bigger fees? Recruiting should not be viewed by the market as a price point solution. It never has been, nor will it ever be. Recruiting should be viewed as a value solution. Yours should be a low-volume, high-margin model. Yours should also be a high-touch model. You are not going to be a company's cheapest solution. But you will be their best solution. Always remember (and remind your clients) that

$$$

yours is predominantly a contingency-based service. You do not get paid unless your candidate is far and away the best solution for the client's needs. If they are not, the client owes you nothing. If they are, however, it should be worth a little more.

Because little things mean a lot.

$$$

Money Maker #42: Can We Talk? No....really....can we?

Communication. That does not mean the same today as it did years ago. Today, communication takes many forms. Text, Email, Facebook, YouTube, Twitter, Instagram, Snapchat, Google+.....holy cow. Welcome to the digital demise! Whatever happened to having a good old conversation....as in verbally....as in talking to people? Verbal communication skills are becoming a lost art. With each generation, those skills are in rapid decline. So if you want to succeed and differentiate yourself from most of your competition, guess what? All you have to do is be able to converse. Digital communication has its place, don't get me wrong. But isn't it ironic that in sales, which is a relationship business, and where all you are supposed to be doing every day is talking with people and gathering information, people have trouble talking. Talking is a skill that is easy to practice and needs no special equipment. And it is a skill that will come in handy when you least expect it.

This struck me during a recent flight I was on from Houston to Baltimore. When I travel, I usually arrive at my departure gate with plenty of time to spare. On this trip, however, that was not the case. First, I got lost driving to the airport (Houston, we have a problem!). Then, there was heavy traffic. Then, there was a long line at airport security. I made the flight, but was the last person on the plane before they pushed back. As a result, I had to take whatever seat I could find ('tis the Southwest way and I usually fly Southwest). I grabbed a middle seat between a young professional and a retiree. Not intentionally, but that's where I landed. The plane pushed back, and the three of us immediately started....talking. And boy was I ever glad I was late for that flight! For the next hour and a half, the three of us talked. And did not stop. We talked about our backgrounds, childhoods, origins, careers, politics, travel, world history, cuisines, sports.....no topic was left untouched. And here's the cool part.....turns out that the young professional seated to my left had a BS in Accounting and was a CPA with Ernst & Young (yes, she got my business card). The retiree to my right had been retired for 15 years and is an ex-McDonald's executive. He worked for the company for 30 years.....starting at their flagship store in

Santa Monica, CA making milk shakes earning $1.75/hour and over the years he worked his way up to a corporate role that focused on global franchise strategy. Now THAT'S climbing the corporate ladder! So one person is beginning her career and deciding if she wants to stay in Public Accounting or make the move to the private side (did I mention she got my business card?) and one person is enjoying the fruits of corporate time well served. Boy was I glad I was running late and got 'stuck' in a middle seat between them.

On that same flight, I looked around at other rows of people. I saw iPods, iPads, iPhones, Kindles, laptops…..people were busy, busy, busy… but no one was talking. What a missed opportunity to discover hidden gems of existence.

In recruiting, we communicate for a living. That is how we are able to forge deep and lasting relationships with our candidates and clients. By talking. And listening. Or at least we should be. Talking and listening, that is. Not emailing. Not Texting. *Talking.* With our mouth. Verbally. Communicating the old fashioned way. *Talking.*

$$$

So, next time you are on a plane, or a train, or a bus, or in line at a sporting event, or anywhere you are surrounded by people, take the opportunity to practice a very important skill - communication. It's something recruiters always need to do. With everyone they come in contact with.

$$$

Money Maker #43: The Pre-Candidate Meeting Email

The initial meeting with a candidate is arguably the most important meeting we ever have with them. There is so much information we need to obtain during that meeting in order to effectively manage, represent, control and close a candidate. Sometimes we find ourselves missing out on basic information that we should always be able to obtain from candidates. Basic information that actually can be obtained before we ever even sit down in front of a candidate.

Prior to your initial meeting with your candidate, send them an email that engages them. Don't just send a confirmation email with date, time and directions. Any recruiter can do that and there is nothing unique about that. However, sending an email that gets your candidate thinking about your meeting with them is. Send them an email that suggests the following:

- Have them mentally prepare for your meeting so they are prepared to discuss career goals, short and long term.

- Set expectations for how long the meeting will last, making sure it works with their schedule.

- Have them make a list of companies they have considered working for (and would not work for).

- Have them make a list of industries they have considered working within (and would not work within).

- Have them reply to your email with a list of references, ideally from a 360 degree view (superior, peer and subordinate) where applicable.

- Bring with them a list of potential referrals that might benefit from our services.

Here is a small example of what such an email might look like:

Dear Katy,

Thank you for taking time to speak with me this morning on the telephone. I am looking forward to meeting you at my office at 7:30am on Thursday, February 28. I have attached directions which

I mapped from your home and work addresses, not knowing which you would be coming from. When you arrive, park in visitor parking and take the elevator up to the 7th floor. Our suite is #721. Our meeting should last no more than 1 hour, and will probably conclude in less time than that, but for planning purposes please budget for 1 hour. I will share information about my company and some of the ways in which we can add value to your career. Additionally, I will be looking to gain a deeper understanding of what is important to you and what you have accomplished thus far in your career. With respect to that, please take some time prior to our meeting to think about the accomplishments that stand out for you. Think in terms of times when your efforts either (a) saved your employer money, (b) made your employer money, or (c) improved processes that made operations in a certain area more efficient. This type of information will help in presenting you to our clients and distinguishing you from others with similar backgrounds. Also, give thought to any industries or companies with which you would like to work (and any you would prefer not to pursue).

In preparation for our meeting, please reply to this email with a list of professional references – peers, supervisors, and, if applicable, subordinates. Finally, if there are others in your professional network who you feel could benefit from our services, please compile a list of those names so that I can network with them, confidentially, in the future.

Should you need anything from me prior to our meeting, please do not hesitate to call or email.

Best Regards,

John

Having all this information prior to meeting a candidate will facilitate discussion and make life easier on you, the recruiter. You will also be able to be more proactive in seeking out possible companies to which you can MPC the candidate.

$$$

Anytime you can make your job easier and have information come to you proactively, you should do it. It saves time. And we all know time kills deals.

Money Maker #44: Add Some Layers to Protect Against the

Counter Offer!

The counter offer. It has long been something recruiters have had to deal with and protect against; and counter offers seem to be occurring now more than ever before. When a candidate accepts a counter offer, it can hurt – often destroy – recruiter credibility in a client's eyes….kind of like how unknown Cinderella teams destroy many NCAA basketball tournament brackets every year…but I digress

I learned something recently that made a lot of sense when it comes to safeguarding against counter offers. Traditionally, even when candidates give us permission to 'accept on their behalf,' I have always had them call the hiring manager (their future boss) directly to verbally accept the position and establish a start date. You may do this now (I hope all of you do this) and it adds a layer of commitment in the process. If the candidate backs out of the deal, they risk burning two bridges – their recruiter AND a hiring manager in their market. This technique of having the candidate call the hiring manager is nothing new, but if you are not currently doing it, please start. It is an excellent best practice. In addition to having the candidate speak directly to their future employer, there is yet another layer of protection and commitment you can add to the equation.

I am a member of the Search and Placement Section Policy Council of the American Staffing Association, and I participate on conference calls where leaders within the recruitment industry discuss market trends and best practices. One of the topics was the abundance of counter offers and how people are dealing with them. One firm in the Southwest does something powerful. Once a candidate verbally accepts to a hiring manager, the recruiter reaches out to some of the candidate's references, shares the success, and asks them to call the candidate and congratulate them. Wow! Now, in addition to the candidate having committed to the recruiter and the hiring manager, they also have peers and supervisors they know and trust calling them to congratulate them. Talk about adding layers! Plus, I thought, this is an excellent way to make additional sales calls to those references – people we may have not otherwise reached out to again.

This is something you should make a best practice. You work too hard to get to the offer stage of a placement cycle. Why not add a few additional measures and layers of commitment in order to maximize your chances for preventing counter offer acceptances? Makes sense to me!

$$$

Money Maker #45: Treat EVERYBODY with Respect....It Will Pay Dividends!

Don't judge a book by its cover. That's a phrase we have all heard countless times over the years, but do we really take it to heart? In our business, first impressions are everything. Often, however, first impressions can be deceiving - especially from candidates. How many times have you walked into an interview room, took one look at your candidate, and thought, "Wow! This person is MONEY!"....only to walk out of the room knowing you could never earn a fee for them. Conversely, how many times have you looked at a resume, spoken to someone on the phone, and thought, "There's just no way I can ever place this person" ...only to finally meet them in person and realize they are spectacular. Those people we initially do not think will amount to much could ultimately end up being extremely successful...they could even end up being hiring managers. Bottom line is, you never know where people will end up. So, a good policy is to simply not cast bias and to treat everyone you meet with the same level of respect. Even when things do not go your way (and often in our world they do not), take the high road and be respectful, not spiteful. It will pay dividends in the future.

I'd like to share two stories with you. One time, a recruiter got an offer for one of their candidates. He, along with several teammates and several people from the client, took him to a very expensive lunch, held his hand through the whole process, and really worked hard to close the deal. The client bent over backwards to get him on board, exceeding budget, giving him a better title…everything possible to get this sought-after, talented resource. A few days prior to the candidate's start date, he called the recruiter and informed him that he was taking another, 'better' offer he had received. The recruiter could have slammed the candidate, gone into a rage, told him he would never represent him again…..and a few other things I could not possibly print here. But he did not. He handled it professionally and treated the candidate with respect. He took the high road. Fast forward a few years. The same recruiter was looking for hard to find talent for a client and

$$$

reached out to this same candidate to source him for referrals. He delivered one and the recruiter placed that person. Being respectful paid dividends.

I read a story once about a gentleman who became known as 'Cadillac Sam' in the Chicago area. He was an emigrant who came to this country with nothing and got a job selling cars in Chicago. One day, a gentleman entered the showroom dressed shabbily and carrying a shopping bag. Not one sales rep wanted to help this person because the first impression did not say much. Cadillac Sam, however, went over to the gentleman, put his arm around him and said, "How can I help you today?" Well, it turns out the shopping bag was full of cash....and the gentleman purchased not one but two Cadillacs that day! Sam did not judge the book by its cover. Sam treated that person with the same respect as he would if the person was wearing a tailored, pressed suit and shined shoes. Being respectful paid dividends.

In sales, and recruiting IS sales, we build a personal brand. People work with us because of who we are....what we are

$$$

about….what our reputation is. Treat everyone you meet with respect, and your reputation will speak for itself. Remember, good news travels fast, but bad news travels faster. And what you put out to the world will come back to you. It will pay dividends. So put out respect!

$$$

Money Maker #46: Set Google Alerts!

Have you ever had a situation where a company you have been trying to do business with finally has an open position you could potentially market candidates to....only you found out about the opening too late? I know I have. It's frustrating. And every time it happens we want to kick ourselves for not being more on top of the situation. For not being more in touch with that company. For not being alerted to the fact that there was a new open position. Well, thanks to the beauty of technology, that doesn't have to happen.

Set Google alerts for companies in your market you are targeting.

It's an amazingly simple thing to set up. Simply do the following:

1. Go to Google.com/alerts

2. In the Search Query box, type the URL of the company's career/job openings page

3. Select 'Everything' for the result type

4. Select 'As It Happens' for how often to receive updates

5. Select 'All Results' for how many

6. Type your email address in the 'deliver to' box

7. Click 'create alert'

If you do this, you will then get an email every time something on the career/jobs page of that company changes....like when they post a new job for example, you will get an alert. Note: it has to be the URL of the *specific page* you want to monitor activity on. The home page of a company's website will not be all encompassing to the entire site.

In our business, when there are tools that can help you improve your operational efficiency and increase your potential for earnings, use it. Google Alerts is one of those tools.

$$$

Money Maker #47: Know Where Your Money Is Coming From!

Money. It is one reason we all entered into the business of sales. In sales, you have control over your income. The harder you work, the more deals you close, the more money you make. Work less, earn less. Make as much as you want or as little (really?) as you want. Either way, you are in control and 100% responsible for your income. Not many professions can offer that luxury or ability. But as we all know, success just doesn't "happen." It takes hard work. And it involves art and science – the latter of which is often overlooked.

You have to know where your money is coming from. You should have a personal income goal each year and that personal goal should allow you to also reach whatever revenue/gross profit (GP) goal your team needs from you (typically your personal goal will be higher, but it should never be lower). After that goal is set – and this can be broken down to a yearly, quarterly, and monthly basis – you then need to determine how many deals you need to close and be a part of in order to attain that goal. Then you have to manage your business accordingly. You have to manage your sales pipeline.

On any given month, deal cycles will have one of three outcomes: (1) The deal will close in your favor; (2) The deal will close, but not by you; (3) The deal will stall and while it still has the potential to close, will drag into the following month. That being said, you are now left with about a 30% chance of closing what is in your active sales pipeline. So…there had better be enough going on in your pipeline in order for that 30% to keep you on track toward attaining your goals. If not, you need to step up your marketing activity and get more job orders to work on so that you can get more send outs. And oh, by the way…even when deals do close in your favor, they too will come off your active pipeline….so you still need to reload. You constantly need to reload your sales pipeline – those activities where you have the potential to make money. Therefore, the only items that go on your pipeline are those activities in which you have interview activity scheduled or is occurring with a client. If you present a resume to a client for consideration, that means nothing. Once they agree to interview a candidate of yours, you have a money making opportunity. Sure there will be some months where you will close more than 30% of your pipeline…and we'll take that! But for accurate forecasting purposes, that 30% number seems to be historically tried and true. So use the science that is available to you and get control of your business. See the sample pipeline below. You need to keep track of all the placement cycles you are involved in and how much revenue/gross profit credit you stand to earn if the deal closes. As an added plus, tie a percentage of confidence to each pipeline activity. This is purely subjective but be honest with yourself. By keeping a pipeline, it helps you clearly see and monitor your business activity. It is also an excellent way to provide forecasting numbers to your management (and a tangible document to back up your numbers).

$$$

Candidate	Client	Fee % / Your Split	Stage in the Process	Est. GP Potential (for you)	% of Confidence it will Close
Name 1	Client 1	25% / 100%	Final Interview	$15,000	80
Name 2	Client 2	22.5% / 50%	First Interview	$7,500	50
Name 3	Client 3	25% / 50%	Offer Pending	$7,500	90
Total				$30,000	
Forecast (30%)				$9,000	

In the above example, the recruiter may have the false

perception that they can book $30,000 in fees for the current month.

However, using the 30% forecasting model, a more realistic picture would be that the recruiter closes less than $10K of business. That's a big difference. If this recruiter wanted to close $30K per month on average, they would need to make sure they had at least $100,000 in potential fee activity in their active pipeline at all times. Makes the eyes open a bit, yes? All the top producers in our business always know where their money is coming from. You should too.

How do we get paid? By delivering to our clients. By closing deals. And in order to close deals, we need to have deals in process…in the pipeline…..so know where your money is coming from. Always.

$$$

Money Maker #48: Audit Your Filled Job Orders!

We don't fill every job order we write. It would be nice if we did, but we do not. Truth be told, on average recruiters probably fill 10%-20% of the job orders they write - (that's 1 or 2 in 10 for those keeping score at home). So what happens with the 8 or 9 that we don't fill? Chances are, (a) we should not have written the job order in the first place, (b) it got cancelled by the client, (c) the client filled it through another recruiter, or (d) the client filled it on their own accord. In (a) and (b), the process is over. In (c) and (d) however, the process has just begun. "But John," you say, "they filled the job and we did not fill it with our candidate, so we're done here….time to move on, right?" Some would say yes. I say no.

Let's talk basic recruiting fundamentals for a moment. When a job gets filled, another job gets vacated. When a job gets vacated, that means that company needs to hire someone to fill that void. Our job is to find out what job got vacated and try to land that job order. This process is what is commonly referred to as a post job order audit.

$$$

So how do we do this? Let's talk recruiting fundamentals

again......ask questions and gather information. Ask your client who

they hired, where they came from (the employer, not the recruiting

firm), why they were chosen, etc. Not only will this clarify why we

lost out on the placement, but, more importantly at this stage in the

game, it will give us a HUGE business development lead. Think

about it....we just spent hours recruiting for a position....we

submitted excellent candidates....we did not get the fill....but they

hired someone of a similar background and now that person is

leaving their employer for a new job....so we need to find out where

they are leaving and immediately make an MPC call to that hiring

manager. AND.... this is where it gets better....we already have

several candidates who fall in line with what the company will need

because we were recruiting for the same profile! We have send outs

waiting to happen! This, my friends, can make you a LOT of

money.

So for all those job orders that are filled by the client or by

another recruiter, get mad that you got beat....and then get busy

$$$

auditing the order and landing a new job order you can fill! Audit

your filled job orders. It will help your business grow!

Money Maker #49: Got Referrals?

Referrals. We all need them. We seek them out. You can never have too many of them. And we never seem to have enough. Finding fee-worthy candidates continues to be one of the most difficult aspects of our job. Yes, there are many passive candidates on the interweb on networking sites such as LinkedIn. Maybe we can even find a few by chance on CareerBuilder or Monster. But how often do we stretch beyond those electronic options? We should end every conversation we have each and every day with, "who do you know?" Do we? My guess is that we probably do not. Maybe it's *who* we're asking. Maybe it's *how* we are asking it. Or maybe it is that we are not asking it at all. It is easy to get short sighted and bail out of a call before doing so, especially if your main objective of that call is achieved. In those cases, don't hang up, hang on. Here are a few things to consider:

- When sourcing for referrals (not references, referrals....there IS a difference), don't ask if the person knows anyone who is looking...or if they know anyone who might want to explore the market...or anyone who might be interested in opportunities. That rarely yields a positive result. Because, as we all know, no one **EVER** knows anyone who is **LOOKING**. But everybody does know *someone*. Be as specific as you can. Ask them who they know or with whom they have worked that performs a specific function. Better yet, ask them for the best person they have ever worked with that performs that specific function. The more specific you can get, the better your chances for getting a referral. Try putting them in a place...painting a picture for them..."at Company XYZ, if you had a question about employee benefits, who did you reach out to" for example. Specific function, specific company. Try it. You'll like it!

- Source management-level references for talent. On these calls, we usually do a good job of *marketing* a candidate to that hiring manager at the end of the call, but how often do we source them for *candidate* referrals? Remember, this is a hiring manager. They have managed people - good people - and we should be asking them who their best employee in a specific function was. Managers love to help the careers of people they have supervised. Don't just market to them, source them for candidates. Again, be specific. For example, "Over the course of your career, who stands out as the best financial reporting person you have managed or worked with?"

- Share a real-life testimonial with your candidate so they can understand how giving you referrals can

  benefit **THEM**. This is a true story you can share with your candidates: One of my former peers was meeting with a candidate. They asked the candidate for referrals so that they could network with them. The candidate provided three names. On a call to one of the referrals, the recruiter uncovered a job order lead. They then followed up on the lead and got the job order...which turned out to be a great opportunity for the candidate who initially provided the referral. This is a great example of how a candidate, without realizing it, can help themselves, not just us, by providing referrals.

- Go deeper into your LinkedIn network. Explore the connections that your connections have. And call them. Don't just InMail them or ask for an introduction. Call them. And source them.

Look for ways to uncover more candidates. Traverse the 'who do you know' network. Talk to everyone in your database, not just the ones who seem right for open jobs. Work your network...I mean *really* work it. You have to touch a lot of hands before you find one you want to shake.

Need candidates? Yes. We all do. Got referrals?

$$$

Money Maker #50: Work on Manager Level Searches!

A recruiter on your team walks into the office and shouts, "New job order - Controller" or "New job order - VP of HR" or "New job order - Director of Marketing" or....ok, you get the point. Someone on your team has just brought in a manager-level job order. What do you do? Hmmm..."I don't have any of them, so I won't work on it" is a response we sometimes hear. Don't be short sighted on this. Manager-level job orders present a HUGE opportunity...and not just for those that fill them. Don't look at it as a daunting task.

With manager searches, it is not about whether or not you have people in your book of business ready to submit. It's about recognizing those searches for the opportunity they present. Every call you make when recruiting for manager-level searches is to a hiring manager. Seize that opportunity and, at the end of your recruiting call to that person, market a candidate to them. Transition that call into a marketing call. Remember...they are currently in a hiring position and although the initial purpose of your call was to try to recruit them, multi-purpose that call…even if you successfully recruit them! It is hard enough to get hiring managers on the phone. When you have them, take advantage of it! And it can be as easy as saying, "Before I let you go, maybe you can help me with something. I am currently working with an exceptional HR Generalist. Whom do you know that would be interested in such a resource?"

When a recruiter on your team brings in a manager-level job order, recruit for it. Work those searches and turn those recruiting calls into marketing calls. The people you speak with can add value to your desk in many ways!

Money Maker #51: Recruit for Talent, not for Open Job Orders!

I went to the store the other day. I was looking for a specific product and, low and behold, they were sold out. The shelf was empty where the product is usually stocked. It is a popular item that people purchase frequently, and this store was out of it. So what did I do? I went to another store, found it, and purchased it. THAT store kept a better inventory of products in demand. In both stores, I also noticed 'gimmick' items that were designed for one-time buyers...going after a specific audience that may or may not always be shopping.

Webster defines the word recruit as, "to gain new supplies of anything." Notice that the word "supplies" is plural. Meaning many. Not just one. In our world, our "supplies" are our candidates, and in order to be in a position to be the best in the market, we need to maintain an inventory of supplies. We need to constantly be stocked up with products (candidates) that are always in demand...and some that are infrequently desired for those times in which they are needed. We have to be prepared for all shopping audiences, so to speak.

All too often when talking with and meeting with prospective candidates, we do so only with a specific job order in mind. And if that prospect doesn't meet what we are looking for, we reject them. We need to think broader - beyond just a specific job order. Recruit for talent, not just for jobs. Always. Remember, our job is to find *talent* in the marketplace. Talent. In general, not just for jobs we are currently looking to fill. So, when you come across exceptional talent in the marketplace, and you do not have anything that falls in line with what they either qualify for or are looking for, don't reject them. Stock them in your inventory so that when a client comes "shopping" you have product you can show them. Better yet, proactively take them to market and create opportunity. Use that exceptional talent profile to secure more job orders.

Keep your candidate inventory fully stocked. Don't just match talent to existing jobs. Recruit talent!

Money Maker #52:   Be Consultative!

"Welcome to our restaurant, can I take your order?" If you have ever been out to eat at a restaurant you have heard these words or something similar. You sit down, a server approaches, introduces himself/herself, and eventually asks to take your order. Some people know exactly what they want, how they want it, and the ordering process is quick and painless. But many times we don't know exactly what we want and we look for guidance. The average server will say that everything on the menu is good and tell the customer they have to decide. However, the experienced, savvy server recognizes this as an opportunity to be different....to add tremendous value...and they make their move. They inform you of the daily specials. They ask what type of food you generally enjoy eating. Then they make recommendations based on your input. More than not, in that scenario, the diner takes the server's recommendation, and the deal is done. It's not always about what the customer wants; because many times, the customer does not know what they want (especially if it is the first time they are dining at that particular restaurant). It's about what the server determines

they are looking for...what they need...based on what the customer

tells them. They work with the customer to arrive at a solution. This

happened to me one time. I was at a wonderful Italian restaurant (go

figure!), and the menu had multiple delicious sounding dishes to

choose from. I was torn. The waiter asked if I had any questions. I

did! At the end of the discussion, he said I would enjoy the veal-

stuffed ravioli. So I ordered it. And enjoyed it. Would I go back

there again? You bet! Food and service were great. And don't get

me started on the wine they served! ...but I digress.

This is not unlike our business. Most recruiters are order

takers. The get a hiring manager on the phone who then sends them

a job description via email, tells them what they want, and they start

recruiting for it, matching candidate skills to the list of skills in the

"required" section of the job description. Ever wonder why all those

things are "required?" Ever wonder if in fact they are

all *really* "required?" What if the client would consider other

profiles? What if the client really isn't sure what they want? You get my point....none of those questions get answered without having a consultative dialogue with the hiring manager. When we ask questions we uncover more information and often find ourselves helping the client decide what they need - kind of like suggesting items off a menu or creating a dish custom for a diner based on what they are interested in having. The more we engage, the more we learn, the more trust we earn from the hiring manager, and the more control we end up having over the placement cycle.

Be different. Work **with** your clients, not just *for* them. Be consultative. They will appreciate it. And they'll come back for more!

Bonus Money Maker #1:   How Many Leads You Got?

Can you ever have enough leads? Leads yield

candidates. Leads yield job orders. Leads yield more leads. Leads

make you money. But if we do not go after them....if we do not ask

the right questions....if we do not take the time to fully probe and

traverse every possible angle for leads....we will not get them. And,

as with most things in our business, it all starts with that first initial

meeting with your candidate. In that initial meeting, we should be

finding out things like:

- Have they submitted their resume anywhere recently? To

  what companies? For what positions? On their own or

  through a recruiter?

- Have they interviewed anywhere recently? With what

  companies? For what positions? On their own or through a

  recruiter? Whom did they interview with (names!)? What is

  the status of their candidacy? Do they know how long the

  position has been open?

- How is their current department structured (have them draw you an org chart)? And the departments at prior employers?

- Who do they currently report to (name!)? And whom did they report to at prior employers (names!)?

- Who at their current or prior employers did a certain function (a skill you need for a job order/search they would not be good for...direct/specific sourcing)?

- How did the candidate find each of their jobs over the past 10 years? Were any through recruiters?

Then comes the real challenge - follow-up. When we get leads, we need to capture the information (usually in a database), act upon them (don't wait!), and then follow-up (set a follow-up task in your calendar or database). And follow-up again. And again. And again. You get the idea. Most recruiters fail in the follow-up department, so if you can continue to follow-up, you have a leg up on your competition.

Clearly, there are many other opportunities when we can gather leads in addition to that initial candidate meeting. But that one meeting can generate a ton...if we ask the right questions. And, of course, the best way you can get leads from candidates is to actually meet with them in person. If you are not meeting candidates in person every day, you are missing out. My recommendation? Meet with 2 candidates per day, 1 active (tons of leads) and 1 passive (fee-worthy). Do that consistently and you will build a great candidate inventory as well as generate more leads than you can imagine. Here's another recommendation....visually track the number of leads you and your team generate. Add a column on your white board for 'leads' and have your team update it daily. If that column is blank or has a zero in it, you are missing out on opportunities in the market.

Ask questions. Get information. Get leads. Follow-up. Make money. Sounds good to me....how 'bout you?

So....I ask you...how many leads you got?

$$$

Bonus Money Maker #2: The Kill Board!

How well do you know your market? Do you know who your competitors are? Do you know where they are doing business? And, more importantly, are they doing business within organizations that you are not? We talk about controlling time and information. Here is yet another piece of information we can and should be controlling – where our competitors are making their money! First, we need to make it our mission to find this out – constantly - with every marketing call and every conversation with active candidates. We need to know who is using recruiters and who is not using us! Then the fun begins…

As you obtain this information, put the names of the companies where your competitors are (and you are not) on a white board in your office. This is not a static list. You will continue to add to it as you uncover these companies which, in fact, become your best prospects in the market. We call this a "kill" board because we are trying to "kill" the competition….one job order at a time! Once you have successfully penetrated one of these companies and made a placement, the company comes off the kill board (or perhaps moves to an area titled "killed"). And of course one placement does not complete the quest. It is but the beginning. We then have to penetrate and mushroom that account to its fullest....perm, temp, department after department. You have to get in first. Then, the sky's the limit.

Kill or be killed. Your choice. Set up a Kill board....it's a great weapon to wipe out your competition!

$$$

Acknowledgements

There are numerous people that merit my thanks. I have amassed a pretty successful career in the recruiting industry (hopefully I have many more years left in me!), but I did not do it alone. No one can, really. So I would like to take a moment to thank those who have truly impacted and influenced my life, both personally and professionally.

First, my wife Lisa. When I left the stable world of software development and jumped into a commission-based recruiting career, she supported me 100%. She has always supported me and there were some long nights and long trips away from home for me while she raised our three children. It takes a special woman to do that. I love you.

Paul Villella, former founder and CEO of HireStrategy, who, after meeting with me for about an hour at a time when I wasn't sure what I wanted to be when I grew up, suggested I consider the world of recruiting. That meeting changed my life. I later went on to work directly under Paul's leadership and learned a great deal from him.

$$$

Paul also believed in me enough to promote me into my first

management position. He has been a close mentor and friend ever

since that first meeting. Thank you, Paul.

Bob Clawson and Jack Causa for taking a chance on a kid

from the Eastern Shore who had no sales experience and who had a

one-way commute to the office of an hour and a half. I told you it

would not be an issue – and it wasn't.

Brendan Courtney who is hands down one of the most

talented and intelligent executives in the staffing industry. I had the

pleasure of working under Brendan's leadership twice in my career,

and I am truly thankful for both of those opportunities. It was

Brendan who initially had the idea of having me craft weekly tips for

our recruiters. It became known as Ruffini's Money Maker of the

Week, the most impactful of which are in this book. Thank you,

Brendan, for your leadership, for the opportunities you gave me, and

for empowering me. Thank you, also, for the indelible memory of

the story of Roger Staubach, which will never fade!

244

$$$

Billy Joel. Just because. I figure his music and lyrics have provided tons of inspiration over the course of my lifetime, so I wanted to take this opportunity to thank him.

Patricia Ruffini who unselfishly spent hours editing this book and made it better. While I may not have included *all* the editing suggestions you made, I did implement each and every grammatical and punctuation edit. Mainly because you threatened me to do so! Thank you.

Finally, I want to thank my father, Anthony Ruffini. Though he is not physically present in this world anymore, there is not a day that goes by where he is not with me in mind and spirit. He is the greatest man I have ever known, and he taught me so much about life, business, leadership, faith, and family. I miss you, dad.

Made in the USA
San Bernardino, CA
15 November 2016